Animations

This catalogue is published to accompany the exhibition

Animations

P.S.1 Contemporary Art Center, a MoMA affiliate, New York
October 14, 2001 – January 13, 2002

Kunst-Werke, KW – Institute for Contemporary Art, Berlin
February 8, 2003 – April 6, 2003

Exhibition:
Curators: Carolyn Christov-Bakargiev in collaboration with Larissa Harris
Directors of Installation: Tony Guerrero for P.S.1, Matten Vogel for KW, Berlin
Animation Consultants: Giannalberto Bendazzi, John Canemaker, Norman Klein and Karyn Riegel
Project Manager: Katrin Lewinsky for KW, Berlin

Web Animation curated by Anthony Huberman
Web Animation environment designed by Paul Johnson
The ABCs of Animation selected by John Canemaker
Hits of the 90s selected by Giannalberto Bendazzi
Edges of Animation selected by Karyn Riegel and Larissa Harris
Folly environment designed by John Pilson and Andrea Mason

Catalogue:
Editor: Klaus Biesenbach
Author: Carolyn Christov-Bakargiev
Managing Editors: Vanessa Adler, Larissa Harris, Anthony Huberman, Katja Morici
Texts: Giannalberto Bendazzi, Klaus Biesenbach, John Canemaker, Carolyn Christov-Bakargiev, Larissa Harris, Anthony Huberman, Norman M. Klein, Karyn Riegel
Idea and Concept: Klaus Biesenbach and New Collectivism
Art Direction: Klaus Biesenbach
Design: New Collectivism

The exhibition at P.S.1 Contemporary Art Center was made possible by the Andy Warhol Foundation for the Visual Arts; MetLife Foundation; Etants donnés; and The British Council.

The exhibition at KW – Institute for Contemporary Art was made possible thanks to the support of Hauptstadtkulturfonds, Berlin

Additional support for the catalogue is provided by Dornbracht Armaturenfabrik, Iserlohn/Germany. www.dornbracht.com

Cover:
Pierre Huyghe, No Ghost just a Shell: Two Minutes out of Time, 2000, video installation with single channel DVD,
Courtesy the artist and Marian Goodman Gallery, New York / Paris
Haluk Akakçe, Illusion of the First Time, 2002, triple channel DVD, Whitney Museum of American Art at Philip Morris
From October 28, 2002 through January 10, 2003,
Courtesy the artist and Deitch Projects New York,
William Kentridge, Shadow Procession, 1999, single channel DVD,
Courtesy the artist and Marian Goodman Gallery New York / Paris

ISBN: 3 - 9804265-0-5

Published by
KW – Institute for Contemporary Art
Kunst-Werke Berlin e.V.
Auguststrasse 69, 10117 Berlin
T. ++49 30 24 34 59-0 F.++49 30 24 34 59-99 email: info@kw-berlin.de
www.kw-berlin.de

Printed and bound in Ljubljana, Slovenia

Available through D.A.P / Distributed Art Publishers
155 Sixth Avenue, 2nd Floor, New York, NY 10013
Tel: 212.627.1999 Fax: 212.627.9484
http://www.artbook.com

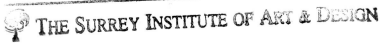

Table of contents

Foreword

The verb "to animate" is derived from the Latin
anima, meaning "life" and the suffix *-ate*, meaning "to give." Therefore, "to animate" is to give
life, or to enliven. The works in *Animations*
endow unlikely objects with unexpected and uncan-
ny life. Some pieces exaggerate their own artifi-
ciality (Sven Påhlsson's slick and thrilling
Crash Course, 2000; Simon Henwood's *Johnny
Pumpkin*, 2000, a Saturday morning on overdrive),
while others openly reveal the details of their
creation (William Kentridge's jagged silhouettes
in *Shadow Procession*, 1999; the elemental figure
in Christina Mackie's *Animated Drawing*, 1999).
The exhibition boasts a diverse collection of
works, including web-based animation, historical
pieces, international contributions to the field
from the last ten years, experimental film-based
animation from New York City, and a subsection of
emerging artists presented on monitors.
Animations, which opened at P.S.1 Contemporary
Art Center in New York in October 2001, was an
important vehicle to enhance and encourage the
public's understanding of a vibrant old and new
artistic medium. I am happy to see this thought-
ful and ambitious show travel to KW, Kunst-Werke
Berlin, where it will, true to the nature of the
medium, take on a new life with new works and
new surroundings.
Thanks to Carolyn Christov-Bakargiev and Larissa
Harris for their tireless work on this important
show, and Antoine Guerrero, Director of
Operations at P.S.1 Contemporary Art Center, for
his invaluable support. Finally, I would also
like to thank the Andy Warhol Foundation for its
continuing support of our programs and its commitment to contemporary art.

Alanna Heiss
Director, P.S.1

10

Introduction

I am proud to present *Animations* at Kunst-Werke, to an audience in Berlin. The exhibition, originally seen in New York, jumpstarts an important cross-continental exchange: artists from around the world are exploring the collective languages of animation and their relevance to contemporary new technologies. Contributions to this artistic dialogue are striking in their diversity and in the variety of their approaches. While many of today's commercial animated images are praised for their computer wizardry, artists have been drawn to the relationships between animation and the more tactile gestures of drawing and sculpting. Artists translate centuries-old art-making techniques into a contemporary language: rudimentary sketches or simple clay figures become moving images and films. Many animators and artists, of course, use digital equipment capable of simulating animated virtual realities, but the technique's conceptual framework lies in the simple architecture of the flip-book. The sequenced frames could be digital or hand-drawn, and it is that flexibility that artists in this exhibition address.

Animation's playful American roots — early experiments in California by James Stuart Blackton became Winsor McCay's cartoons and Walt Disney's 1928 Mickey Mouse trademark — were mirrored by innovative techniques and aesthetics in Europe, particularly in Oskar Fischinger's abstract work from the 1920s to the 1950s. Animation has come to play a central role in today's popular global imagination, and the artists in this exhibition explore those shared memories — American, European, Asian and beyond.

This exhibition showcases the unique ways in which contemporary visual artists address animation as a medium and subject. *Animations* focuses on the implications of living in an age where visual experience is informed by new technologies, and where the "reality" of live action film and the imagined worlds of animation have been blurred. The exhibition addresses the utopian beginnings of the medium, the relationship between analogue and digital, between graphic form and 3-D animation, and between commercial and experimental animation.

Techniques include Karen Yasinsky's stop-motion clay figures, William Kentridge's combination of live action film with drawing, or Pierre Huyghe and Philippe Parreno's ready-to-use digital *anime* character purchased from a corporate agency, which references the anime version of Masamune Shiro's comic story, *Ghost in the Shell*. In addition, the exhibition provides audiences with opportunities to connect these projects with the broader context of animation: historical animation programs, film-based hits of international animation from the 1990s, and a program of experimental New York animators are screened continuously. Web-based work — a significant new development in the way artists are addressing animation — is included as well. An archival space with dozens of works by emerging artists has been designed by John Pilson and Andrea Mason.

The exhibition was realized through an unwavering faith in the collaborative process. P.S.1 Director Alanna Heiss's encouragement was crucial to me and to the entire exhibition team. Curator Carolyn Christov-Bakargiev worked closely with Larissa Harris to select the works. Artists Gareth James, John Pilson, Andrea Mason, and Paul Johnson each played a central role in the exhibition design. Anthony Huberman selected and developed the web animation section. John Canemaker, Giannalberto Bendazzi, Norman Klein, and Karyn Riegel lent their expertise and contributed texts to the catalogue. I am indebted to all of them, as I am to my staff at Kunst-Werke, in particular to Katrin Lewinsky, Exhibition Manager, Matten Vogel, Technical Director, and Katja Morici and Vanessa Adler, Publications. My most sincere thanks go to the Berlin based Haupstadtkulturfonds, which supported this exhibition generously.

Klaus Biesenbach
Chief Curator, P.S.1
Artistic Director, KW

Texts

Animazione povera: Towards a Theory of "Poor" Animation

We live in an age when visual experience is informed by new technologies and its imagery: slick, moving graphics and volumetric, gloppy shapes that seem alive in games, on TV, at the movies, on the web. With new computer software, the "realities" of live action film and the imagined worlds of animation have blurred. But it seems more important today to create cartoon-like imagery than to "imitate" the real, even though that has become technically possible. Producing ever-more sophisticated "artificial" images expresses a sense of power over the world, a power similar to that of decoding the genome. This exhibition juxtaposes works by artists and animators who raise questions about this contemporary cultural condition. Is animation a realm of freedom, as it was traditionally for historical animators, or of pornographic spectacle? Is animation today a Frankensteinian pursuit that produces monsters and commodities in a globalized world? Has animation invaded our architectural space to the point where theme parks are our model homes, stores and museums in new forms of "architainment"? Is cartoon imagery appropriate for interaction between distant players in multi-user games? Is animation still the way to express the complexity of knowledge today, its layered and overlapping nature, the slippages, loops, interferences and disjunctures of repetition and difference, and the relations between the brain and the mechanical product? Self-referentiality pervades the exhibit. It is animation about animation. Although incorporating the digital, it is not an exhibition about new media. It brings together artists working with the "hand-drawn" and artists using digital processes.

Apparently unrelated, all are fascinated with movement and metamorphosis, and all explore fantasy worlds that cannot be captured by photography or film from the real. This exhibition embraces the utopian beginnings of the medium, when animators did not erase their own traces in a quest to imitate life. It also explores the relationship between analog and digital, between graphic form and 3-D animation, between commercial and experimental animation, and between the experimental animation done in the film world and the "meta-animation" conceptual works by contemporary visual artists. Some of these works look at the collective memory of animation and cartoons — how watching Looney Tunes, Walt Disney films and, more recently, Japanese *anime*, can shape a consciousness where fiction and fact overlap and perception and memory collide into imagination. Some works exacerbate the possibilities of popular animation to the point of satire — as in Simon Henwood's work. Some, like Haluk Akakçe, recall the Baroque and the supernatural. Others, such as Francis Alÿs, resist the high-tech digital aesthetic of much current 3D animation by suggesting early vaudeville gags or, like Karen Yasinsky, by returning to stop-motion animation that focuses on characters' interactions and fractured and ambiguous narratives. Such practices seem to question the fascination for high-tech animation and point to a form of "poor" animation that expresses the need for intimacy, simplicity, and basic phenomenological and "low-tech" approaches to experience. They are created slowly, anti-efficiently, absurdly. William Kentridge is known for his technique of filming single frames of drawings, altering them through erasure or addition, so that each image retains traces of a previous frame. The film becomes a moving palimpsest of experience, memory and consciousness. Kentridge's *Memo* (1993–94) is a collaborative work made with Deborah Bell and Robert Hodgins, where the artists join film from the real with paper props and link an actor with drawing: a business-like figure draws his own desk in a humorous reflection on authorship and self-referentiality. It combines live action film with drawing and recalls the beginnings of animation at the turn of the last century. For the exhibition in Berlin, Kentridge has chosen to project *Shadow Procession* (1999) which depicts a haunting procession of black puppet-like figures made from cardboard cutouts. A unique and new set of drawings, *Untitled (video reversals)* (2002) explore the shift from animation to still drawings. On the other hand, French artists Pierre Huyghe *(Two Minutes out of Time,* 2000) and Philippe Parreno *(Anywhere out of the World,* 2000) have created video-installations that address the contemporary corporate context of much animation today through the "plight" of Annlee. Annlee is a ready-to-use *anime* character that Parreno and Huyghe purchased from a Japanese cartoon agency for their international project "No Ghost, Just a Shell," through which the artists have "saved" Annlee from imminent disposal by the *manga* comic industry. The "episodes" of "No Ghost, Just a Shell" are part of a collaborative project to which other artists — such as Dominique Gonzalez-Foerster and Liam Gillick — have also added episodes, up to Annlee's recent and symbolic "death" through fireworks on a beach in Miami in December 2002. Like a rumor or a virus moving through the art world, this project addresses collective consciousness and questions individual authorship, as each new artist contributed an "interpretation" of Annlee. It also

proposed the liberatory possibility of constructing a narrative oneself, or with a group of friends, even in our corporate world.

The exhibition is a curatorial hybrid, bringing together artists' installations incorporating animation as well as micro-exhibitions within the main exhibition: a folly/arcade of single channel works the audience can view as if looking through an archive of animation works in a TV environment; a space for web animation; a paper laboratory space where different artists' works are contaminated by each other; and a screening area that recalls the "cinema" experience where various programs of animation, both from the history of the medium and from contemporary sources are presented.

Some of the artists refer to the collective memory of cartoons — an animistic world of fiction laden with violence, deep psychological impulses and the recollection of childhood: Juan Muñoz' *Waiting for Jerry* (1991), redesigned by the artist for this exhibition in New York in 2001, is a dark room lit only by a small mouse-hole in a corner. Once inside, the viewer hears a collage of sound effects from the cartoon that suggests moments of violence — crashes, punches, etc. As you listen, childhood memories are triggered, and the passion, humor and violence of laughter and drama emerge in a poetic, theatrical environment. *Waiting for Jerry* is a metaphor for escape, an escape from the endless roll of images, an escape into the radicality of cartoons. Muñoz was working on this project when he suddenly passed away. I would like to dedicate this exhibition to his memory.

Carolyn Christov-Bakargiev
Chief Curator, Castello di Rivoli
Museo d'Arte Contemporanea, Turin

Animations
(a guide for the novice)

Animation is interesting to focus on now because it's one of the places where contemporary art practice bumps up against the film tradition. This juxtaposition illuminates both worlds, and may be a useful jumping-off point for understanding the goals of this very diverse exhibition. There are a few different kinds of animation-practitioners in *Animations*. First, there are the artists who have made only one project involving animation: who chose, found, or bought moving images and used them as tools to analyze and reveal the place those images hold in society. For *Every Anvil*, 2001, New York-based artists Jennifer and Kevin McCoy subjected 50 Looney Tunes to an extreme form of Propplike structural analysis, cataloging and grouping together every falling anvil or every silhouette escape. These super-recognizable moments make up a language and, *Every Anvil* points out, our familiarity with this language forms a huge part of our pleasure in cartoons.

The artist-collaborators on *No Ghost Just a Shell* (1999–2002) purchased a young female *manga* character from a Japanese *anime* firm, gave her a new voice and personality, and then made her available to other artists to re-create and/ or ventriloquize. Each re-embodiment refracts our relationship with corporate entertainment and spectacle culture back to us — slightly altered — through Ann Lee's inescapable pathos (which itself stems partly from the fact that she's a young female, a Galatea). At the same time, each contribution is perhaps less important than the overall project's process of dissemination of an open(ed) sign. (The individual works by Philippe Parreno, Pierre Huyghe, and Liam Gillick can be seen in the exhibition at Kunst-Werke; other artists involved include Henri Barande, Francois Curlet, Dominique Gonzalez-Foerster, Pierre Joseph with Mehdi Belhaj-Kacem, M/M Paris, Melik Ohanian, Richard Phillips, Joe Scanlan, Rirkrit Tiravanija, and Anna-Léna Vaney.) These works' relationship to the film or animation tradition resides in the way they reflect on it as an institution or a language.

Then there are people who have chosen animation as their primary medium. They fall into two categories: those who identify as artists and those who identify as filmmakers (a partial list of the artists would include Haluk Akakçe, Jeremy Blake, Simon Henwood, Angus Fairhurst, Sven Påhlsson, Liane Lang, and William Kentridge). Though the works of, for example, Karen Yasinsky and Liliana Porter — both primarily self-defined as artists — recall the persistent self-reflexivity and Modernist roots of the work featured in the experimental animated film program "Edges of Animation" (as pointed out in Karyn Riegel's essay in this publication), differences between the two forms and their relationship with narrative run deep.

Experimental film — to make an egregious generalization — is in a sort of perpetual Oedipal struggle with its narrative origins. The contemporary artist's parallel move away from the static image has led her towards a flirtation with narrative. But even though Karen Yasinsky's stop-motion films contain all the elements of narrative — men, women, tears, and travel — in the end, they consist of a mood, not a story. It's the "difficulty" in the telling that makes those stop-motion tears, when they come, all the more potent. Similarly, Liliana Porter's solitary toys set off thoughts of a world of play-acting and story-telling, but have been restricted to a single mechanized movement over a few sugary seconds. Despite thirty years of the phrase "breaking down boundaries," Yasinsky's and Porter's work (and work by those artists listed above) continues to display the characteristics of their lineage in art.

We can focus on differences between the works on display for the purposes of laying out an understanding of the exhibition; but then, perhaps, we can abandon this attitude. All of the work has an emotional content and a relationship to magic that is impossible to ignore. Industry animators (from Warner Brothers to K-Works) and the people working on the fringes of film throughout the twentieth century have always known about this relationship, and have created a world whose fertility and complexity contemporary art has recently begun to acknowledge and analyze.

Larissa Harris
Independent curator and editor, Artforum.com,
New York City

On the Web

Moving beyond technical feats and "interactive" puzzles, web-based art is ageing well. While the visual interface of the world wide web has existed for all of eight years, artists around the world have nudged and pried open its multi-disciplinary potentials. Graphic designers, sound artists, creative writers, and visual artists have combined the soft sculptures of computer software with the social sculptures of computer net-works. Fitting in a variety of art historical lineages, from Joseph Beuys to John Cage, artists working on the internet have incorporated contemporary culture's digital impulses and addressed the implications of an emerging artistic medium. This exhibition attempts to present certain backbone characteristics of what it means to work with animation on the internet and to categorize some of the most significant and clearly defined strategies: interactive, multi-user, and standalone.

Many artists take advantage of the user-driven nature of the internet. A significant interactive system that many artists have uncovered is the animated game. As artist and game designer Eric Zimmerman says, "games are among the most ancient and sophisticated forms of designed interaction," and artists have learned to combine this nostalgic appeal with difficult conflicts and unresolved relationships. Natalie Bookchin's *The Intruder* recounts a violent short story by Jorge Luis Borges through *Pong* and *Space Invaders* game formats, forcing the viewer to playfully implicate him/herself within an aggressive language of jealousy. Panajotis Mihalatos's *Flexible Planning* makes a maze out of the infinite variations inherent in the binary relationship of all things digital and lures users with a flexible modernist grid. More Op than Fluxus, Mark Daggett turns web pages into bleeding watercolored paintings: his *Blur Browser* animates each page by having it slowly go blurry, while retaining its full functionality. Mouse movements cause the colors to blend and swirl, enabling users to create their own brand of abstract expressionism with their favorite site. Mouchette's *Lullaby for a Dead Fly* also teases mouse movements as an innocent click leads the viewer to a stream of medi-

tations on death and fragility contributed by past visitors to the site. Choosing the key-board instead of the mouse, Golan Levin and Casey Reas's *Dakadaka* empowers users to compose a symphony of animations to the rhythm of their typing of letters.

Multi-user environments are the playgrounds of the internet. Chat rooms set up around the many talents of Hollywood actors or of Playboy Playmates take up countless hours of countless lives. Bringing animation to such a complex platform is a challenging task, yet contemporary online habits have bred a culture of simultaneity and community, and artists are finding in multi-user animated environments a way to satisfy and further explore that sense of immediate digital proximity. Setting up a frame, successful projects leave it to the users' movements, decisions, and fantasies to animate the screen. In an immensely popular multi-user game, Eric Zimmerman and Word.com's *SiSSYFIGHT 2000* combines the aesthetic of early cartoon animation with real-time interactive fights in a schoolyard. Often without the resources to create such intricate environments, other artists find quieter ways to animate the screen. Only across the web would it be possible to create an animation out of a blank canvas. Along with Mark Napier's *p-Soup*, Andy Deck's *Open Studio* is literally that: a blank canvas on which logged-on users draw and scribble, adding and subtracting in real-time to their "collaborative" drawing. The process translates the realities of a networked culture into animation, a culture where no image can be static and no movement invisible. John Klima urges online users to share and mix sound files in a 3-D musical instrument called *Glasbead*. Interested in hybrid visual-audio-interactive experiences, the artist has created a context for users to animate compositions in real time. In each case, it is in the artist's absence that the animation builds.

The internet's most persistent virus is the somewhat abstract requirement for interactivity. Dismissing the commonly-held belief that the web is the 21st Century's answer to interactive art, many net artists present their "users" (as the web audience is invariably called) with unclickable, and therefore often unsettling, interfaces. One of the best examples of these stand-alone applications might be YOUNG-HAE CHANG HEAVY

INDUSTRIES's *DAKOTA*. An aggressive animation made up of bold black words, flashing by just slightly too quickly, tells a disjointed story of a Homeric suburban journey towards death and alcohol, based on poems by Ezra Pound. Not getting a word in, users are silenced and immobilized by the endless sequence of exclamations. Interaction screeches to a halt and gives way to an animation unforgiving in its pace, volume, and font size. Xeth Feinberg's *Bulbo* also uses the black and white aesthetic and suggests the relevance of old-fashioned cartoon strips in digital space. In another instance, Sebastian Luetgert does the web-surfing for you: simulating the unique proximity between websites, with AOL one click away from Adidas, his *Coils of the Serpent* reduces the process of navigating the internet to a sped-up series of animated corporate logos and accentuates the user's inability to contribute. As artists and computer programmers, Alex and Munro Galloway prefer to have real-time weather conditions instead of greedy and impatient users trigger their animation. In *Day In, Day Out,* an algorithm locates the computer's geographical location, gathers real-time weather data from online sources, and translates the information into a computer-generated image of a partly clouded sky. The artists use the internet in a way that can never be interactive and the almost imperceptible animation reflects that which no user can program: real-time changes in weather patterns. Almost mimicking art history's trajectory from the inanimate (painting, sculpture, photography) to the animate (film, video), net art has gone from MUDs and MOOs, to HTML, to Flash, Shockwave, and Java, to algorithms turning real-time data into dynamic visual landscapes. Of course, while online moving images have not replaced static ones, artists have found a variety of ways of joining and pursuing the collective memory of animation. Partial as much to the Looney Toons as to Pierre Huyghe, web-based animation reaches across cultural backgrounds, aesthetic traditions, and art-making strategies. What all of these projects have in common is the internet, always open-ended, relentlessly wavering between public and private, formed and formless, visible and invisible.

Anthony Huberman
Director of Education and Public Programs, P.S.1

Animation: Painting with a Machine Gun

Increasingly, animation is invading architectural space, since the opening of Disneyland in 1955, and along the Vegas Strip. And in themed spaces of all kinds: animated monsters inside stores, at rock concerts, as interactive merchandising, in military simulators and in target sights, for museum exhibitions and art installations. This adaptability should hardly surprise us. Even in Melies' trick films, we sense a very old form of animation in the staging, as if Melies' were archiving something going back to the Baroque. In much the same sense, miniature sets of early Starevich animation refer back to table-top illusions centuries old. Clearly all movie miniatures bridge that older system, where graphics and architecture meet. And now, animation seems to be everywhere in the consumer-driven city, like a Disney store winking at us.
But film theorists have a problem calling such a wide range of phenomena animation, even if historically they are. But that is hardly a surprise: as a meta text, animation is generally ignored, along with its links to sculptural and graphic allegory, to folklore, illustration, slapstick, Baroque pageant, puppet animatronics (Baroque robotics). Why then should animation in architecture be noted, in Bernini, in seventeenth century theater? At the same time, more architects are using systems of animated space, what in Las Vegas is called architainment. And every movie set begins as architainment — walk-through animation — before it passes through the camera lens. We know that special effects are fundamentally animation; and that movie editing is rendered increasingly like special effects.
Animation suddenly becomes a vast issue (architecture, cinema, consumer theming, etc. I'll call the sum of it "archi-animation." That will be easier to read, fewer over-inflated clauses (ridiculous to say out loud, but helpful as text). Then I can introduce archi-animation systematically but briefly — its sources, structures, and rhythms:
Sources: What is the difference between "archi-animation" and live-action cinema? For that, we imagine ourselves in a conversation three hundred years ago. In the room is a primitive form of moving picture — the optical lantern (later called the magic lantern). It had been invented,

for the most part, by the scientist Christian Huygens, then advanced by that eccentric Jesuitical polymath, Athanasius Kircher. However, even by 1700, the optical lantern was archi-animation: sculptural graphics animated by light. What's more, there was a philosophy for what I am labeling archi-animation, well known among engineers, artists, architects, and philosophers. Generically, archi-animation was called an "engine," or a "machine." These were essential for theatrical illusions (like the masterful flying devices of the Italian master, Giacomo Torelli).

Thus, a philosophy of archi-animation, as of 1700, might go something like the following: an engine (that is archi-animated) makes the spiritual look magically solid. It reminds the viewer that Spirit is merely echoed in what is solid, like sculpture, automata, etc. These engines revealed what was called neo-Platonic. And neo-Platonic can be science or pageant. An archi-animation comes to life, but stays a machine. Its sculptural illusions (like Baroque CGI, like mechanized trompe l'oeil) works on the eye like a ladder — a Jacob's Ladder, an Axis Mundi. This ladder bridges the gap between the material we can touch, and the invisibility of God. A piece of sculpture is animated to remind us that God breathes through all things. Thus, animation is animism, to show you your place on the ladder. ("Your place" is essential here. Archi-animation was supposed to defend the monarchy and the church, as it defends globalized capitalism today. But that problem takes us far beyond a brief introduction. Reluctantly, I merely point out how politically cautious archi-animation tends to be. I'll leave an ellipse here (…), as if it were five pages long, about biting the hand that feeds you.)

Story Structure: Archi-animation was structured around a device that was called "artifice." That meant the pleasure of seeing nature is invaded by artifice, by human craft. Thus, it was structurally necessary for archi-animation to reveal its falseness, as well as its ergonomic sense of comfort. A brilliantly crafted engine entertained like a trapeze act; it emphasized the high wire, the floating ceiling. We saw "man's fragility" before the mysteries of the numinous, before the powers of prince and the church. Of course, artifice has an etymology all its own. By the middle of the eighteenth century, the neo-Platonic defense engine had sub-divided into separate

fields — into mechanical science, magic, mesmerism, tricks with optics, and what eventually became cinema.

Rhythm: For that, let us jump forward to the late twentieth century. The charm of artifice — coming out of films as puppet theater — is epitomized by the animation of Tamas Wilitzky. Special-effects films had regenerated the neo-Platonic paradox, with a pacing that reflects consumer-driven entertainment. And the fine arts have embraced archi-animation in their own way, first as industrial bricolage, classically in the mathepoesis of Duchamp's Great Glass. Let us simplify that for clarity's sake: industrial artifice as neo-Platonic paradox. Over the past forty years, the rhythm has sped up, to match the changing of the guard: digital, global, etc.

Thus, rhythm here points toward the media that dominated material culture at the time — and their political power. In recent years, a new crop of museum installations features automata and animatronics, to suggest that this power has gone digital: digital miniaturization invades more fiercely year by year. The engine for neo-Platonic artifice becomes the body itself — nanomation. FX as artifice: animatronic aliens look uniquely perverse when they are still unfinished, when their metallic limbs are not yet covered in prosthetics, as if they were golems about to awaken. The movie itself as urban planning: now we essentially eat inside the movie set, visit cities staged like a movie set. Archi-animation has surely gone to the highest bidder — as global capitalist fantasy.

But it also remains perversely intimate. Archi-animation is an inside/outside pilgrimage, the artifice of the real micro-edited into no space at all. No wonder animation continues to obsess young artists. Its neo-Platonic journey can so easily be updated for the entertainment economy, as anti-product design. I often call animation "painting with a machine gun." Archi-animation can sell practically anything, including salvation. It can make wars look cute (The Gulf War), make shopping almost pornographic. It can build cyber-surveillance for the whole family. It fits easily into any mode of globalized fascism. And it is arguably the most personalized — and critical mode — of cinema imaginable (neo-Platonic pleasures frame by frame).

Norman M. Klein

Professor, California Institute of the Arts

Plus Ça Change...

Animation, unruliest of art forms, currently eludes description and classification boundaries, thanks to digital imagery's blurring the distinctions between film and animation. During its century-plus history, animation — now an inescapable part of nearly every communication mode — has continually absorbed, hybridized, mutated, and melded other disciplines (dance, music, graphics, painting, sculpture, text, acting, etc.), merged techniques (pencils to puppets to pixels), and attracted both commercial exploitation and artistic exploration.

In the current exhibition, one finds links to older creators, films, techniques, and styles by new artist/animators. Self-consciously and not, they are finding fresh ways to stretch the expressive and emotional borders of animation and its definition.

William Kentridge's compelling *Memo* explores animation's potential for magical metamorphosis and startling juxtapositions. He is infused with the same spirit of discovery and delight with the medium as were pioneer animators James Stuart Blackton, Emile Cohl, and Winsor McCay. Kentridge uses substitution devices (a clock becomes a live man's face, for example) and a live actor interacts with cartoon imagery, as did Blackton in 1908 in *Humorous Phases of Funny Faces*, the first known frame-by-frame film of drawings.

The earliest "trik-films" experimented with technique, but were basically a technological magician's act geared toward light entertainment. Kentridge probes deeper using his tricks (including a pre-cinema flipbook of a cartoon nude) to describe the tediousness of a man's daily life, the boring, pompous office tasks that collapse an entire day and literally kill time. Aggressive paper work, official stamps and signatures threaten to overwhelm the man (and finally do) blackening his hands and face (an apt "dirty business" metaphor). Swallowed up by mind-numbing minutia, Kentridge's man exists in an out-of-control cartoon world recalling Max Fleischer's *Ko-Ko's Earth Control*, a 1927 Out-of-the-Inkwell short.

Karen Yasinsky's stop-motion short *Still Life w/Cows* contains technical and emotional echoes of Ladislas Starevitch's 1912 puppet short *The Cameraman's Revenge*. The latter film depicts a love triangle melodrama in the insect world: a hotel tryst between a comely dragonfly and a philandering beetle photographed by a vengeful grasshopper cameraman who later screens the erotic "documentary" publicly.

Starevitch's anatomically correct craftsmanship of the amorous bugs is impressive, and the surreal-looking characters move tentatively with minimal pantomimic expressiveness. Ms. Yasinsky's puppets and settings contain painstaking craftsmanship — in *No Place Like Home* she reproduces the poppy field set from MGM's *The Wizard of Oz* — and an almost painful lack of animation (or motion) technique. The halting, slow, clumsy, unspecific movements of her mute puppet characters contributes greatly to the films, which deal with unresolved, conflicted relationships, sexuality, and memory. The slow, non-narrative, anti-animation approach draws the viewer into the films, and contributes to the pervasive sadness, ambiguity, tension, anxiety, and inarticulate longing.

Simon Henwood's slickly-made computer series *Johnny Pumpkin* is an over-the-top parody of big studio animation — specifically the personality-driven narratives, overly-detailed designs, and family-audience merchandising tie-ins of the Walt Disney studio and its computer arm Pixar. Like John Tenniel on acid or a techno-Bosch, Mr. Henwood throws so much plot and so many bizarre characters at us, we drown in his toxic, saturated colors and convoluted, ultimately nonsensical narrative — something to do with a blue-sky future world polluted by greedy corporate villains and personified, lethal hiccups who battle assorted innocents, including robots, odd-looking children, and draffes: gentle Shmoo-like creatures whom the kids casually torture.

Jeremy Blake's saturated color abstractions stem from a long line of west coast "visual music" animators, such as Oskar Fischinger and the Whitney brothers; Melissa Marks' mischievous, invisible character Volitia unfolds her "dramas" like a Chinese scroll painting, the original animation "storyboard"; Philippe Parreno and Pierre Huyghe purchased a ready-to-use character — the miserably depressed Annlee — and put her into videos that parody Japanese *Manga* and *Anime* and provoke questions about identity, self-esteem, and art versus life.

The artist/animators in *Animations* pour new wine into old bottles and recognize (as did their forerunners) animation as the art form that truly brings ideas to life. They prove that the brave new world of animation lies not in techniques, but in new approaches to this most malleable and exuberant of the lively arts.

John Canemaker
Acting Chair, Film & Television Department,
New York University

THE ABC'S OF ANIMATION
Selected by John Canemaker

James Stuart Blackton, *Humorous Phases of Funny Faces*, 1906

Emile Cohl, *Fantasmagorie*, 1908

Winsor McCay, *Little Nemo*, 1911

James Stuart Blackton, *The Haunted Hotel*, 1907

Winsor McCay, *Gertie the Dinosaur*, 1914

Walt Disney, *Mickey Mouse and Steamboat Willie*, 1928

Tex Avery, *A Wild Hare*, 1940

Chuck Jones, *Duck Amock*, 1941

Len Lye, *Trade Tattoo*, 1936

Len Lye, *Free Radicals*, 1958

James Whitney, *Lapis*, mid-1950s

Oskar Fischinger, *Allegretto*, 1943

Caroline Leaf, *The Street*, 1976

Norman McLaren, *Begone Dull Care*, 1949

Peter Foldes, *Hunger*, 1974

Faith and John Hubley, *Moonbird*, 1959

A Tribute to Robert Breer: Robert Breer, *A Man and His Dog out for Air*, 1957; *66*, 1966; *70*, 1970; *77*, 1977

Nick Park, *The Wrong Trousers*, 1995

The Sounds of Motion

Animation is a deceitful art form. To explore its intellectual geography and in particular its language dead-ends and borderlines might be, for a scholar, as fleeting and probably as romantic as reaching for the roots of the rainbow — in other words, it would mean to see the destination endlessly move away. Nowadays, animation par excellence (or rather, its best-known branch) is the TV series, be it Japanese (anime) or American or even European. Aesthetics has normally little to do with it, and gives way to sociology, mass psychology and media studies. The film critics covet theatrical feature films. Then what about the shorts made by the independents, about the commercials, about the video-clips, about the avant-garde films, and so on, and so on?
Most people think of animation as a film genre, something I consider to be a mistake. A genre is based on the guarantee that that specific show will meet some specific and generally agreed-upon expectations. If you want horses and revolvers, you take a western; if you want to laugh, you take a slap-stick comedy. We have all learned, in our youth, that a pear, an orange, or a pineapple are different, but that they each satisfy that expectation of freshness, taste, and substance that we call "fruit." If a fan of Japanese *anime* watches Yuri Norstein's masterful "Tale of Tales," he will feel sorely disappointed; those addicted to "Beauty and the Beast" will hate abstract films; Bugs Bunny and Droopy will collide with Eastern European aphoristic short comedies. In fact, what we have to do is to think of animation cinema as a cinema of its own: the live action cinema's twin brother. The lesser-known baby of the magic lantern and the photographic device. It is a lesser-known old being whose name itself will probably change once the current film prints, theatres, and markets fade away. It is certainly not always, probably not at all, lesser. It boasts a parallel history, parallel genres, auteurs, technologies, a star-system, festivals, gurus. It is quite odd that in the year 2001, more than a century after the first hand-drawn scenes were screened to an audience (by Emile Reynaud, in 1892, at the Musée Grévin in Paris), these words aim at introducing animation to the reader. On the other hand, I have for decades been experiencing so many misunderstandings, even in the most cultivated circles, that I feel too much zeal is better than no zeal at all. In fact, animation's output has always been badly-viewed because it's been badly distributed

(does a market for the short subject exist at all?), and is still undermined by the people (almost invariably strongly self-ironic people) who are actually making their bread and butter out of it.

I am extremely pleased that art and animation meet each other and go shoulder to shoulder in this exhibition. They are no less correlated than animation and cinema. Think of kinetic art on one side, think of painted-on-stock films on the other.

I do believe another misunderstanding is worth clearing up: animation is certainly the art of the moving image, the invention of motions and movements, and the choreography of drawings and shapes. Were it only that, however, it would remain a specialized branch of kinetic art. Indeed, animation's specific physiognomy is the most audio-visual of the audiovisual languages. Animated characters, or patterns, or colors have always aimed at a marriage with music. Score specialists such as Carl Stalling, Raymond Scott or Normand Roger have always conceived music in its broadest and most contemporary sense — notes, noises, voices, or any kind of sound. Try screening a "Wile E. Coyote vs. The Roadrunner" film without its soundtrack, and it loses all its power and meaning.

This synesthesia is what animators can award our spiritual, emotional, and intellectual inner world. It pursues the ageless human aspiration to harmony and immerses the viewer in a multi-sensual experience. Animation in this sense dates back to Pythagoras, it was developed in the 19th century by the Symbolists, it has accompanied us through the century we recently left behind us, and today's widely popular version pulsates every night with the flashing lights of disco clubs.

Giannalberto Bendazzi
Animation Historian

HITS OF THE 1990S IN THE WORLD OF ANIMATION
Selected by Giannalberto Bendazzi

Piotr Dumala, *Kafka*, 1991
Caroline Leaf, *Two Sisters*, 1990
Michaela Pavlatova, *Repeat*, 1995
Alison Snowden and David Fine, *Bob's Birthday*, 1993
Wendy Tilby and Amanda Forbis, *When the Day Breaks*, 1999
Seriy Vol and Garri Bardin, *Grey Wolf and Little Red Riding Hood*, 1990
Alexandra Korejwo, *La Traviata*, 1995
Alexandra Korejwo, *Season*, 1995
Daniel Greaves, *Manipulation*, 1991
Jerzy Kuciz, *Tuning the Instruments*, 2000

The Animated Reflex

Reflexivity is perhaps the most essential impulse in both classic and contemporary experimental animation. After all, animation is the after-image of material truth and chimerical optics: single frames in rapid succession fuse into a kinetic illusion made in the mind's eye. While frame-by-frame construction is the obscured basis of most filmmaking, it is a conscious activity to the animator, who crafts each still frame as a fraction of cinematic time. Perhaps this heightened awareness of process can explain why self-referentiality surfaces as a perennial subject in animation. The history of studio production recalls the pre-modern painter's quest to achieve realistic perspective. Through inventions such as the rotoscope, the cel process, and digital modeling, animation erased its own traces and evolved as a fantastic imitation of life. But even studio auteurs revealed their artifice in fleeting winks: Otto Messmer sketched the brush that brings *Felix the Cat's* very special tail to life; the animator's hand appeared physically in The Fleischers' *Koko and Bimbo* cartoons, and figuratively in Chuck Jones's *Duck Amok*.

While the anthropomorphism of Bugs Bunny became increasingly conventional, artists of an often-overlooked tradition approached animation as an art of anti-illusion, using its methods to explore the stuff and subjects of film itself. Born at the heights of Modernism, this reflexive impulse — the graphic cinema — grows out of a preoccupation with the formal and material dimensions of cinema. Painters-turned-animators began working with the medium to take the ludic, lyrical, and conceptual extensions of Cubism and Neoplasticism into the realm of the moving image: Hans Richter's *Rhythmus* series rarified image as a fluid matrix of geometric forms; Len Lye scratched intricate kinetic patterns directly onto film stock in *Free Radicals;* and Robert Breer took montage to an atomic level of fragmentation with single-frame manipulation in *Recreation.*

Today, the "digital revolution" continues to transform the production and aesthetics of consumer-oriented animation, and simulations threaten to dissolve the division between illusion and photographic reality. The industrial promise of celluloid's extinction has catalyzed a return to the graphic fixation on film's material properties, evident in the hand-painted abstractions of young filmmakers such as Jennifer Reeves and Sandra Gibson. Many media artists continue to awaken our critical awareness, recasting cinema's mesmerizing spell by probing the implications of animation as a mass cultural phenomenon and as part of the broader history of the moving image. Questions of representation and language guide Peggy Ahwesh's *She Puppet*; appropriating images from the video game *Tomb Raider,* Ahwesh leads a conceptual adventure through interactive fantasy, feminism, and masochistic identification with virtual pop icon Lara Croft. With cutouts culled from 1940's *Cosmopolitan,* Lewis Klahr reconfigures stargazing, consumerism, and fashionable nostalgia in *Altair,* a near-narrative critique of glamour and decadence. Soaked in similar shades of *film noir,* Janie Geiser's intricate *Lost Motion* utilizes playthings, found artifacts, and mundane objects as part of an oneric deconstruction of melodramatic cliches, children's games, and unrequited desire. Reflexivity is also at play in the mainstream: remember how Roger Rabbit and the other Toons were framed as secondary citizens in tinsel town, a repressed minority of celebrities relegated to kiddie entertainment.

A simple narrative of animation might sketch an evolution from primitive plasticity to mimetic agility, from analogue to digital, from —ism to individuality, and set up a binary between the artist's savvy and commercial fantasy. On the contrary, we encounter an organic constellation of styles, values, techniques, and aspirations: an anarchic medium, a vast expanse of the collective self-conscious.

As Robert Breer suggests: "…time doesn't move forward, things *are* going, but sideways, obliquely, down and backwards, not necessarily ahead. The sense of motion is the issue. That idea seems hard to defend, because our locomotion drives us forward with our faces looking at new things. But since that movement is toward oblivion, in my philosophy anyhow, it might well be backward. It's a delusion to think you are getting anywhere."

Karyn Riegel
Program Director,
Ocularis Cinema Williamsburg Style

EDGES OF ANIMATION
Selected by Larissa Harris and Karyn Riegel

Jeff Scher, *Milk of Amnesia,* 1992
Janie Geiser, *Lost Motion,* 1999
Jenn Reeves, *The Girl's Nervy,* 1995
Emily Hubley, *Pigeon Within,* 1999
Lewis Klahr, *Altair,* 1994
Sandra Gibson, *Soundings,* 2001
Rachel Mayeri, *The Anatomic Theater of Peter the Great,* 1999
Julie Murray, *Domain,* 1999 (sound composed by Jed Distler, performed by Margaret Lang Tan)
Luca Buvoli, *Not a Superhero,* 1997
Devon Damonte, *Catcycle,* 2001
Emily Breer, *Superhero,* 1995

Haluk Akakçe

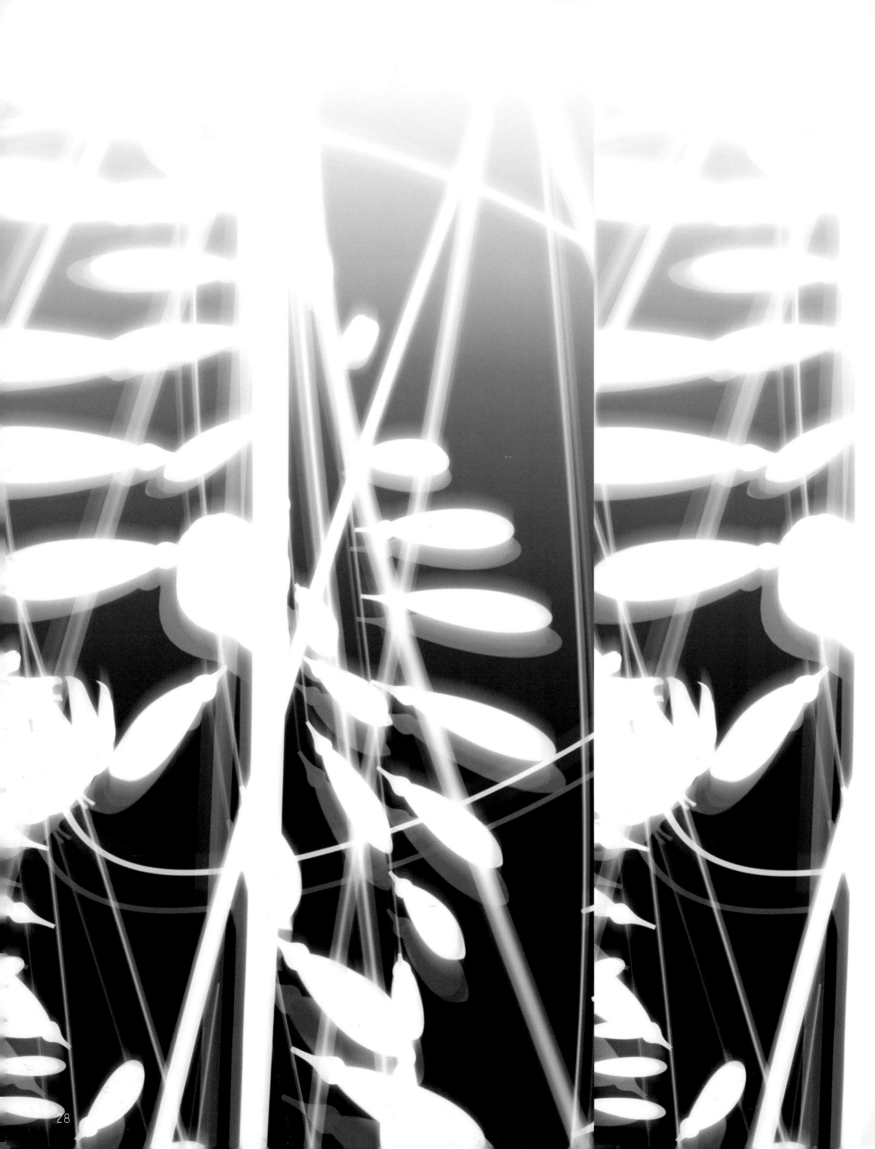

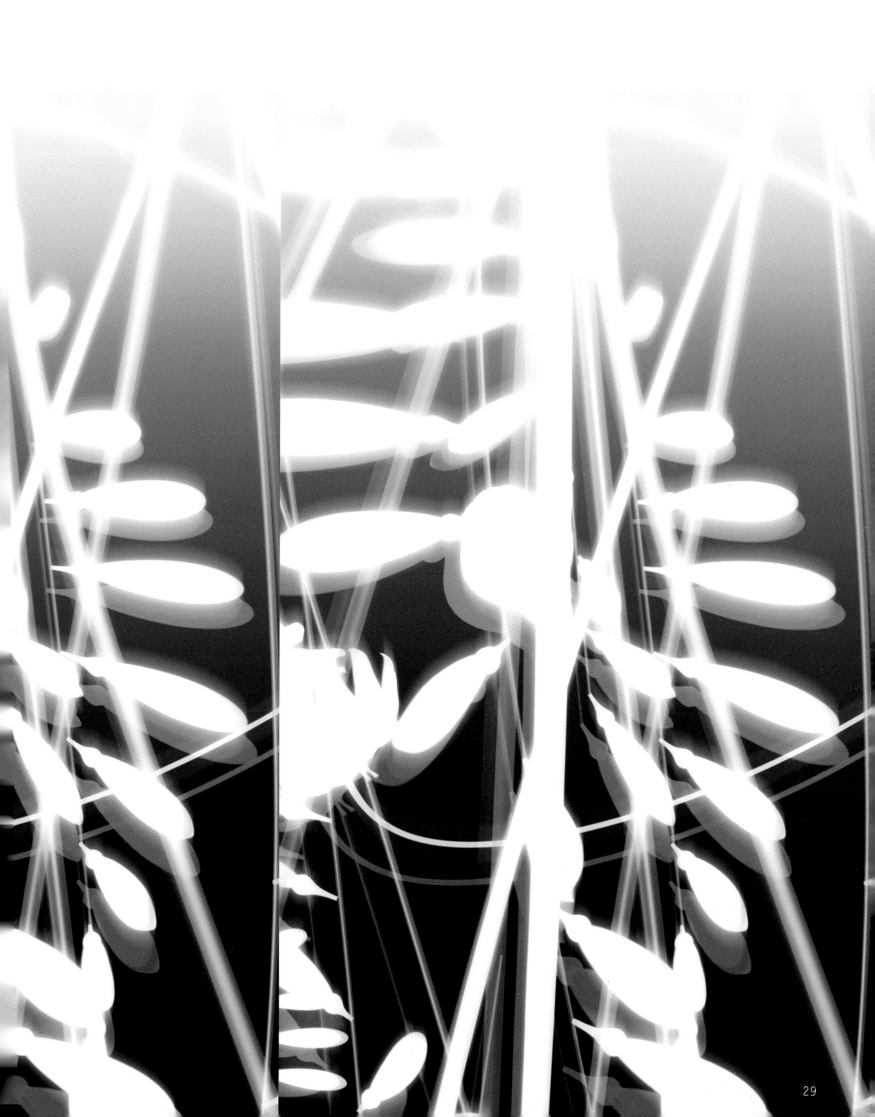

Francis Alÿs

40

41

No Ghost, Just a Shell

Pierre Huyghe
Philippe Parreno
Liam Gillick

50

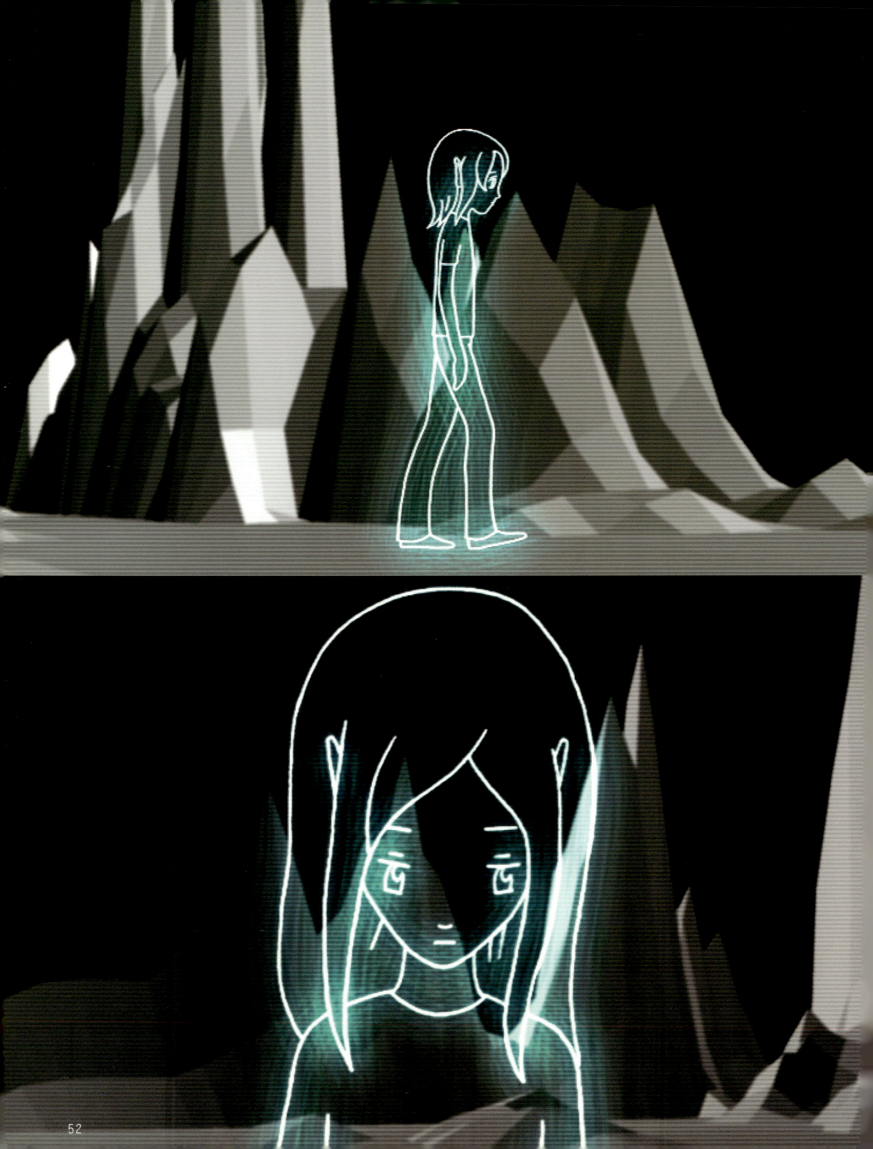

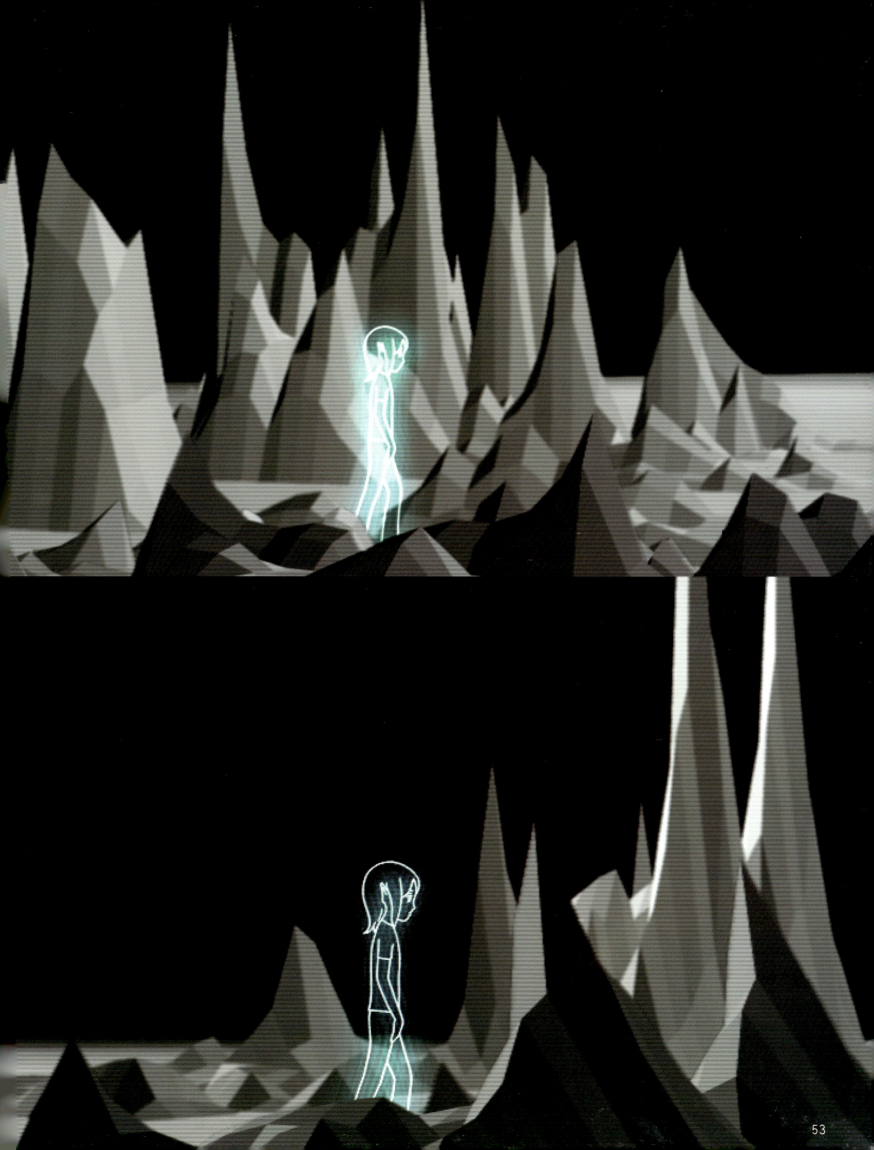

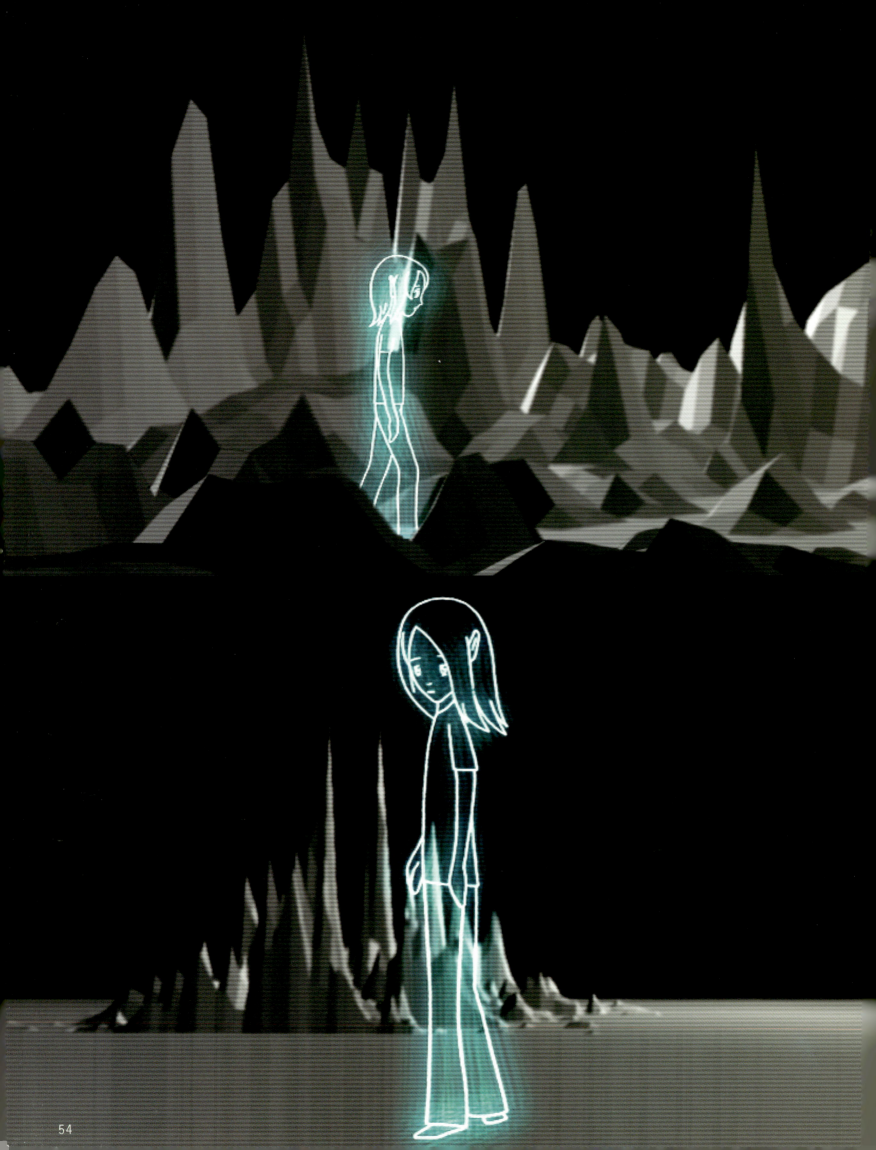

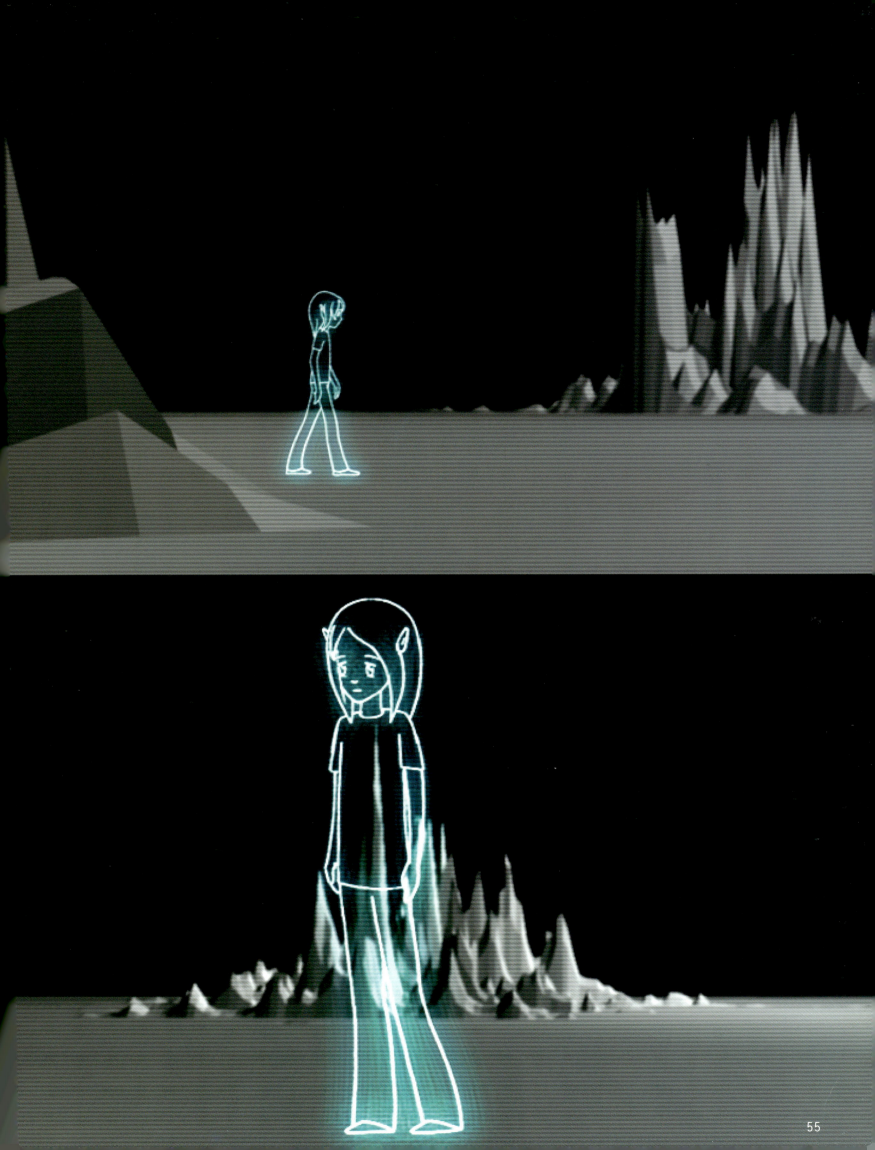

55

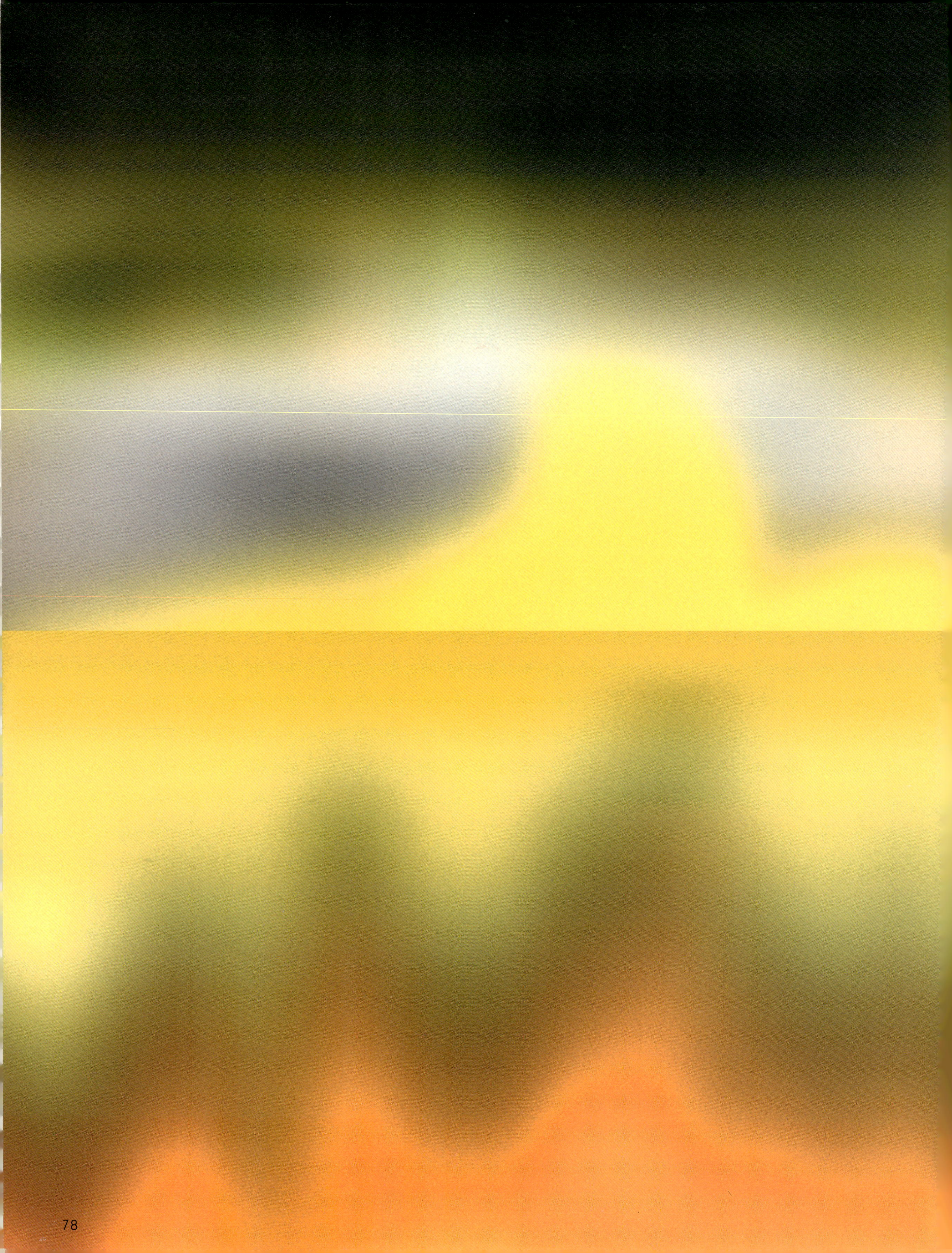

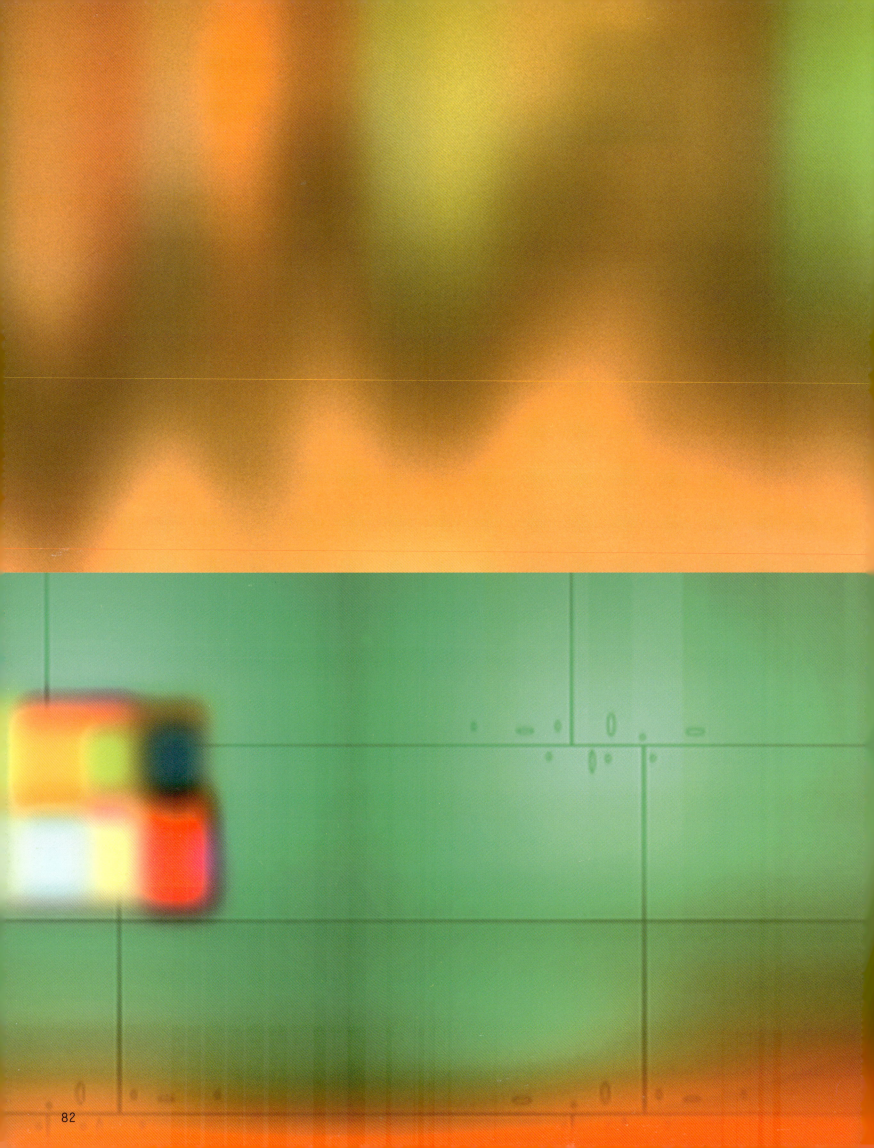

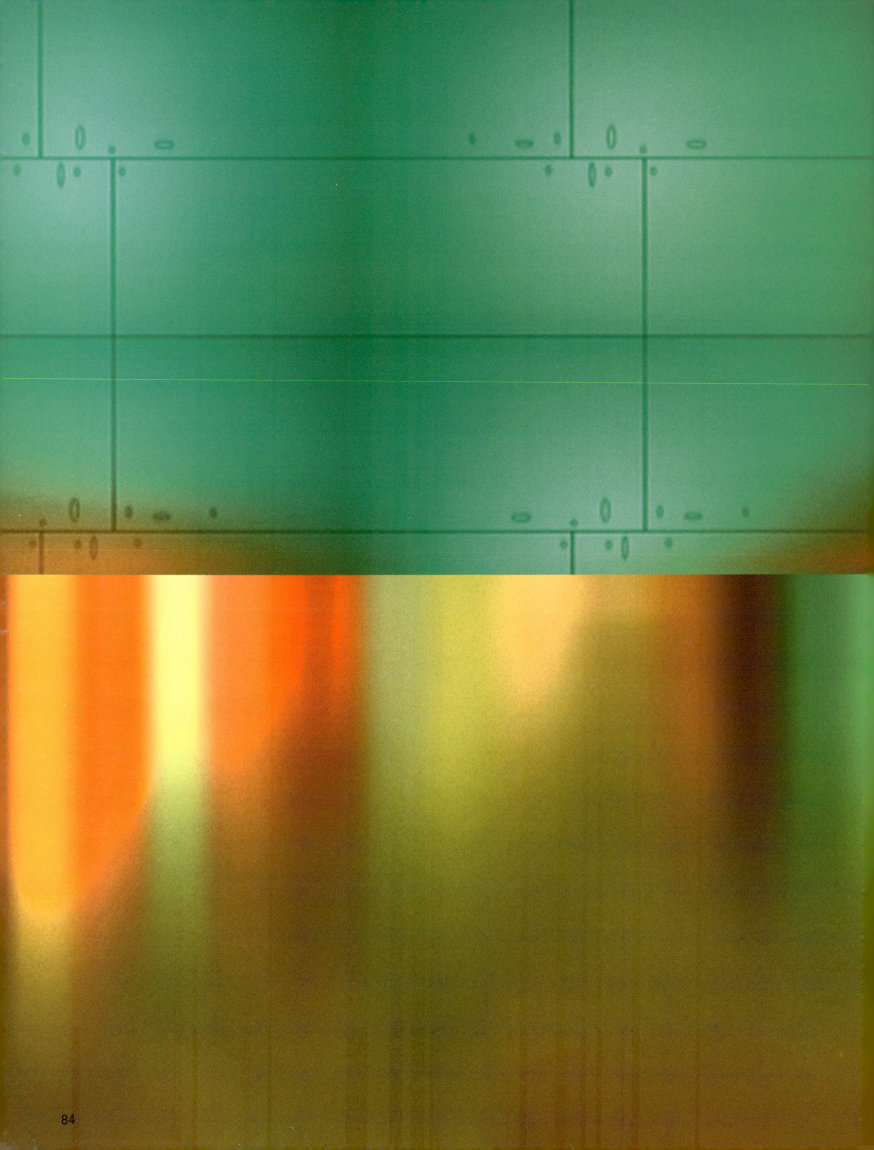

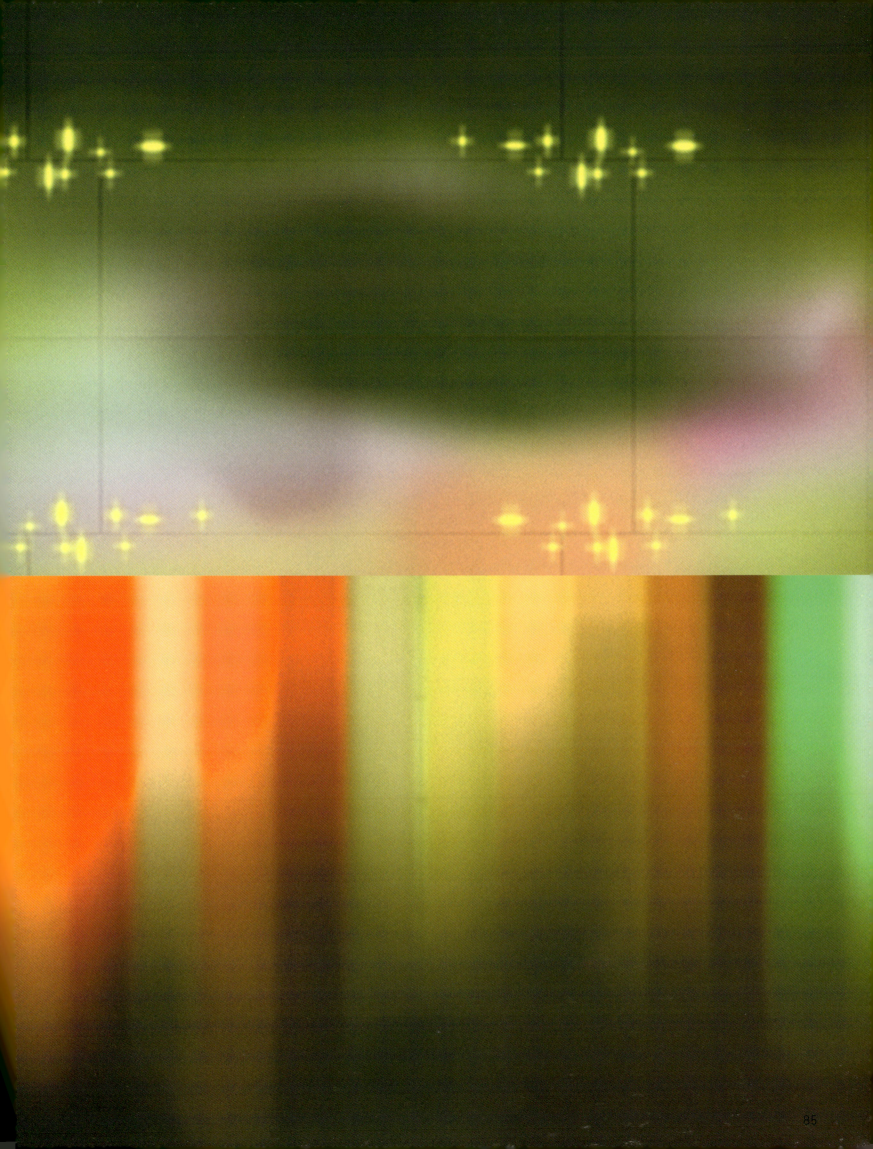

Karen Yasinsky

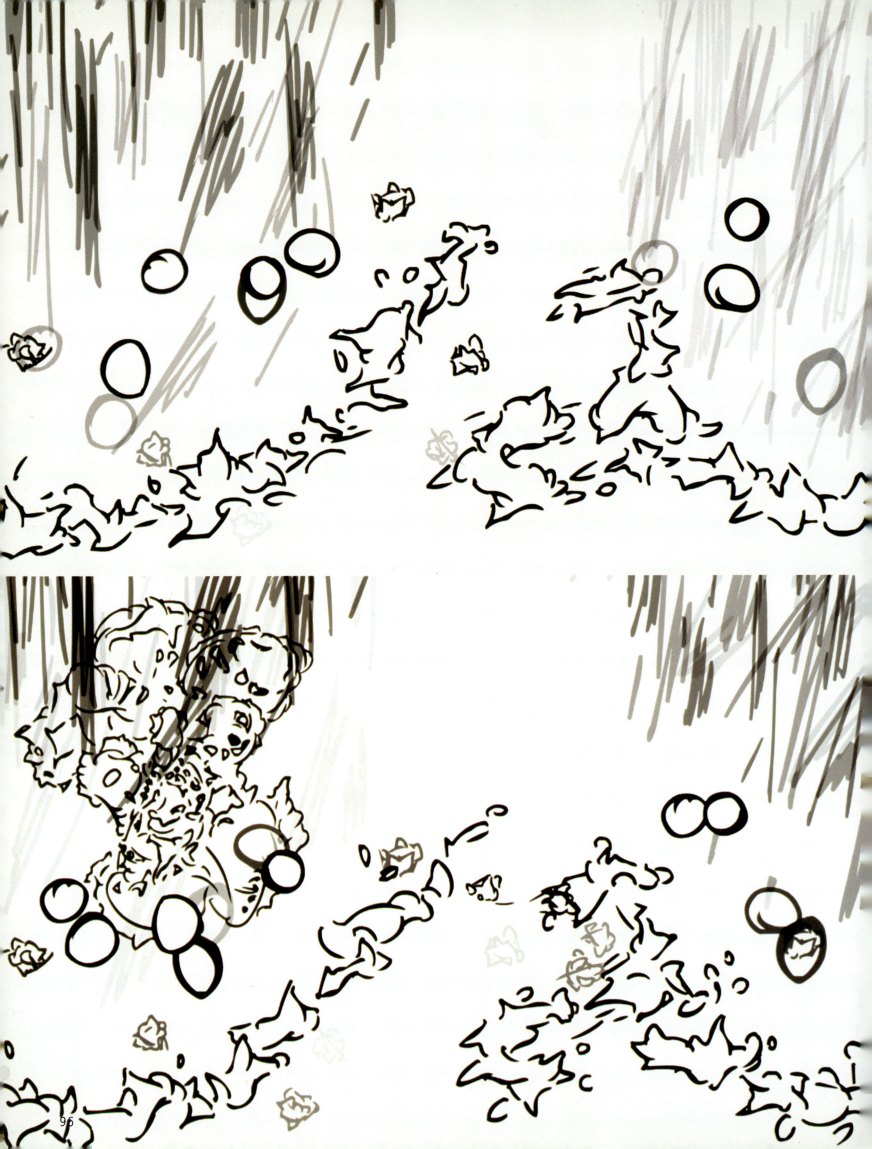

William Kentridge

103

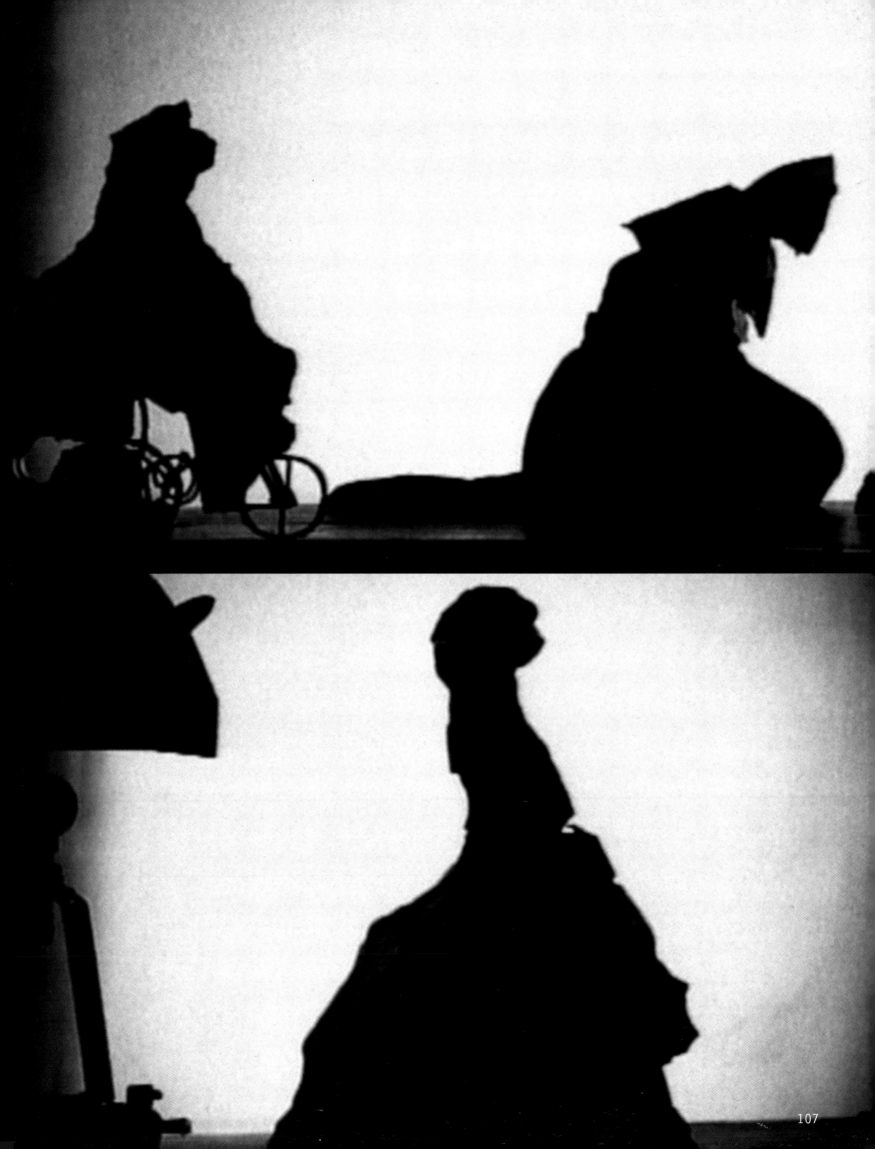

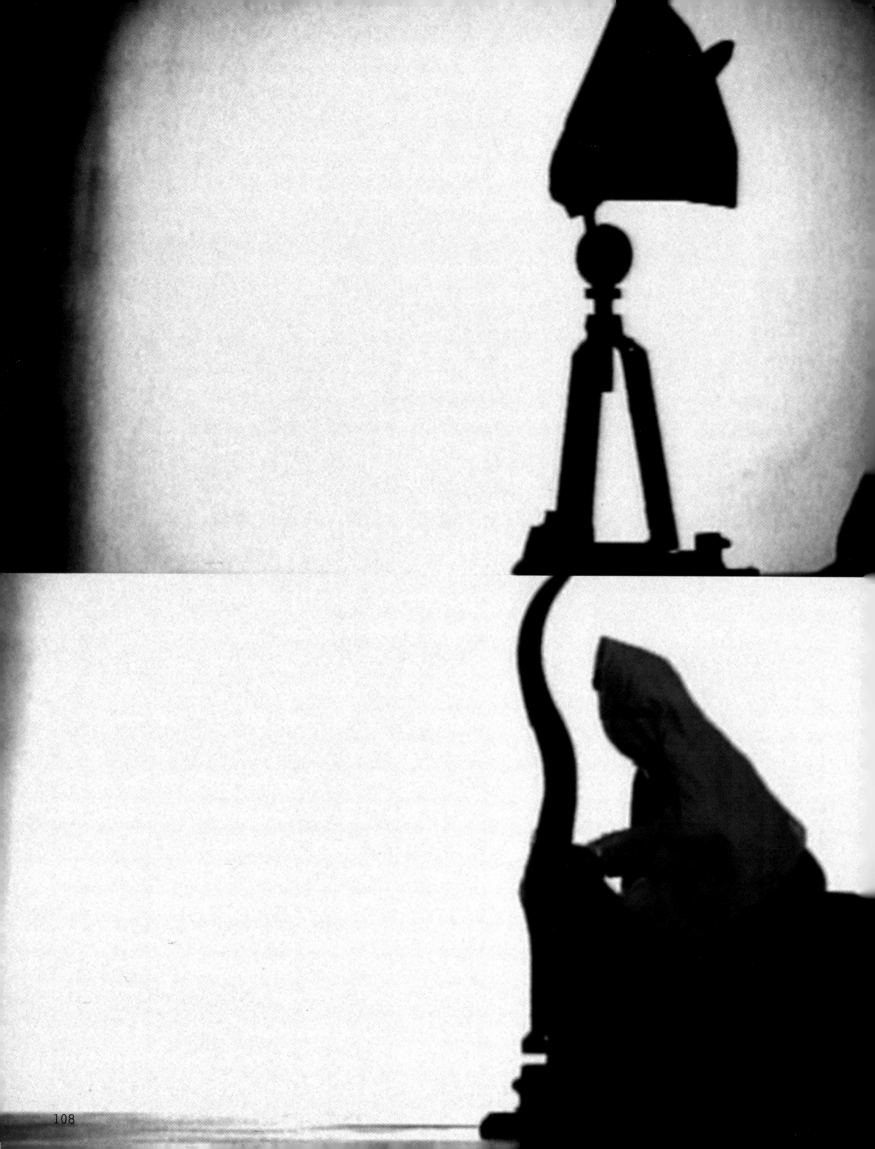

114

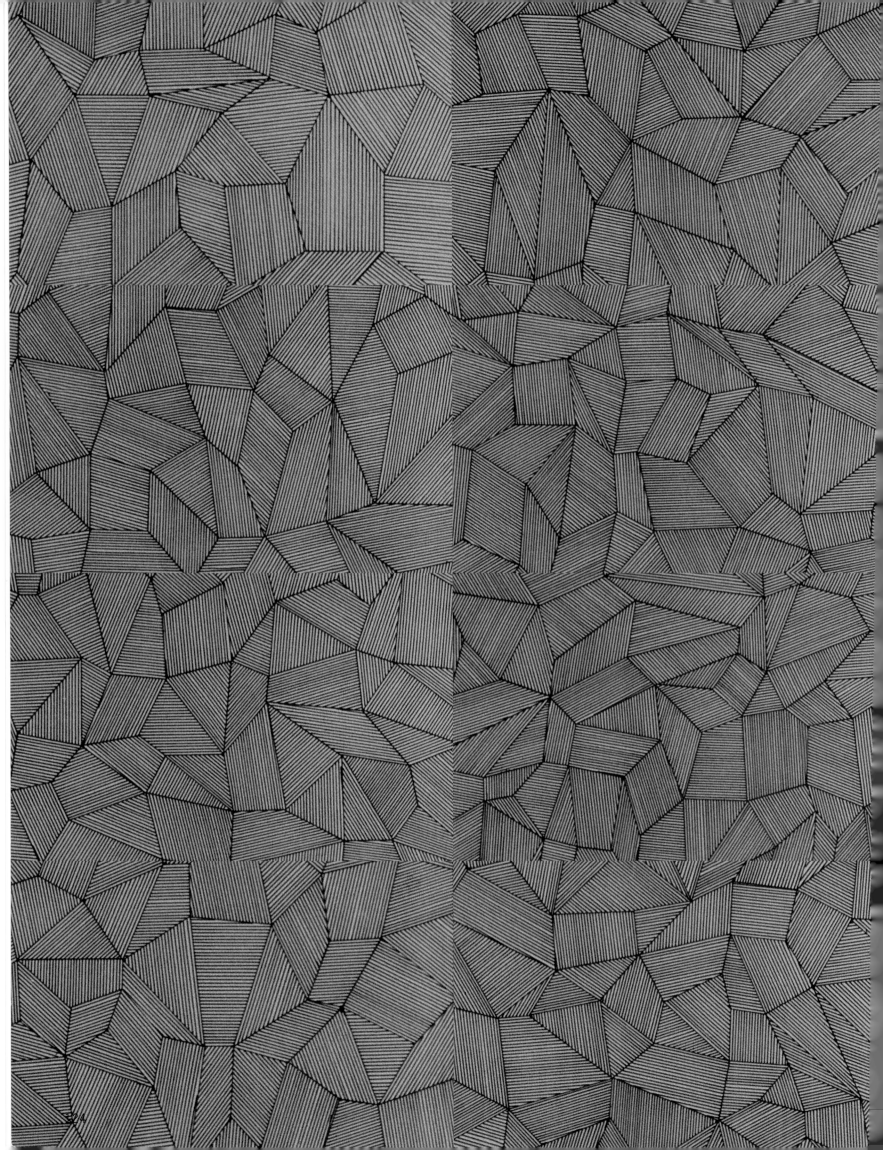

PICTURE
START

ooks

ERMA

PICTO

OOSI

126

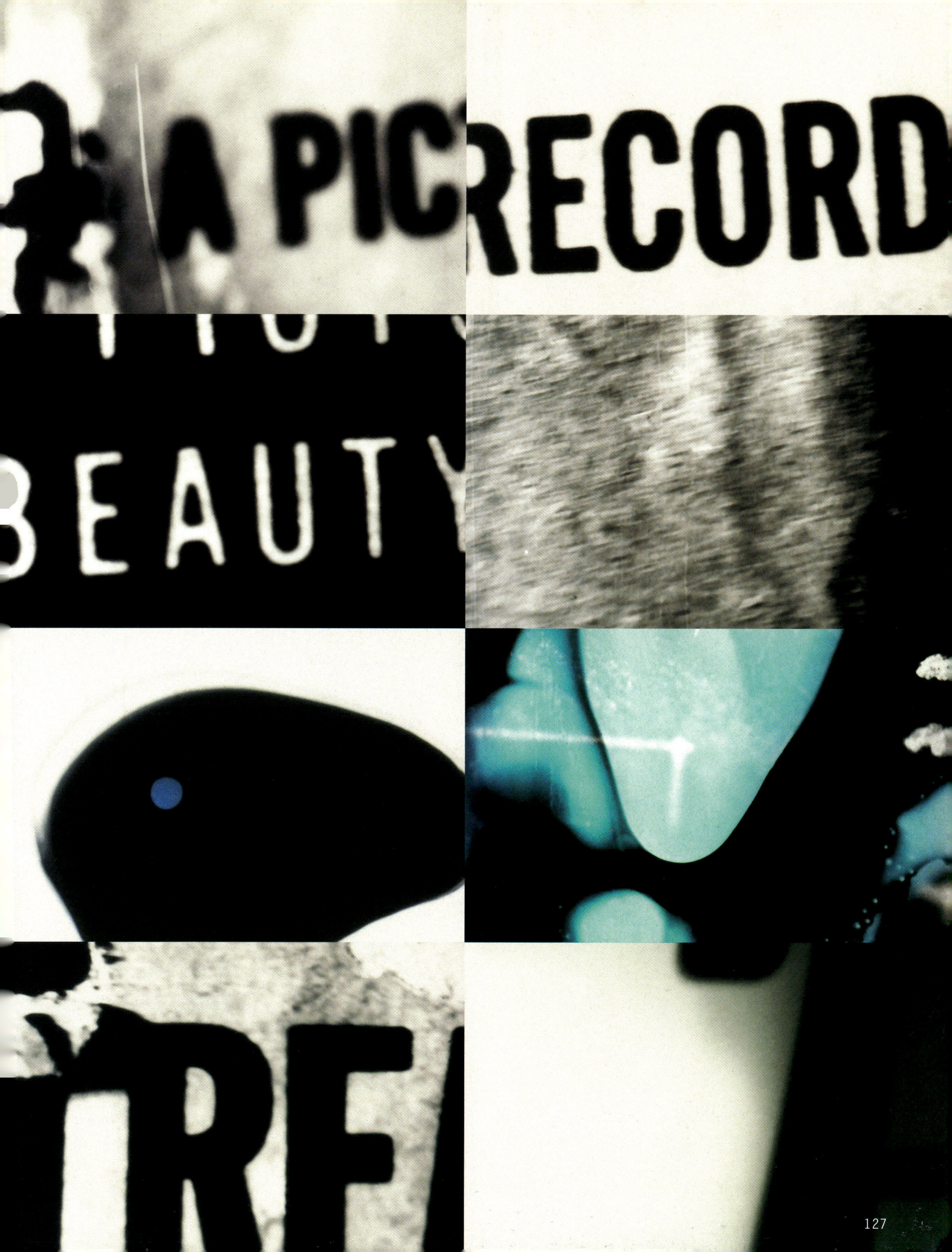
A PIC
RECORD
BEAUTY

Simon Henwood
Peggy Ahwesh
Liliana Porter

131

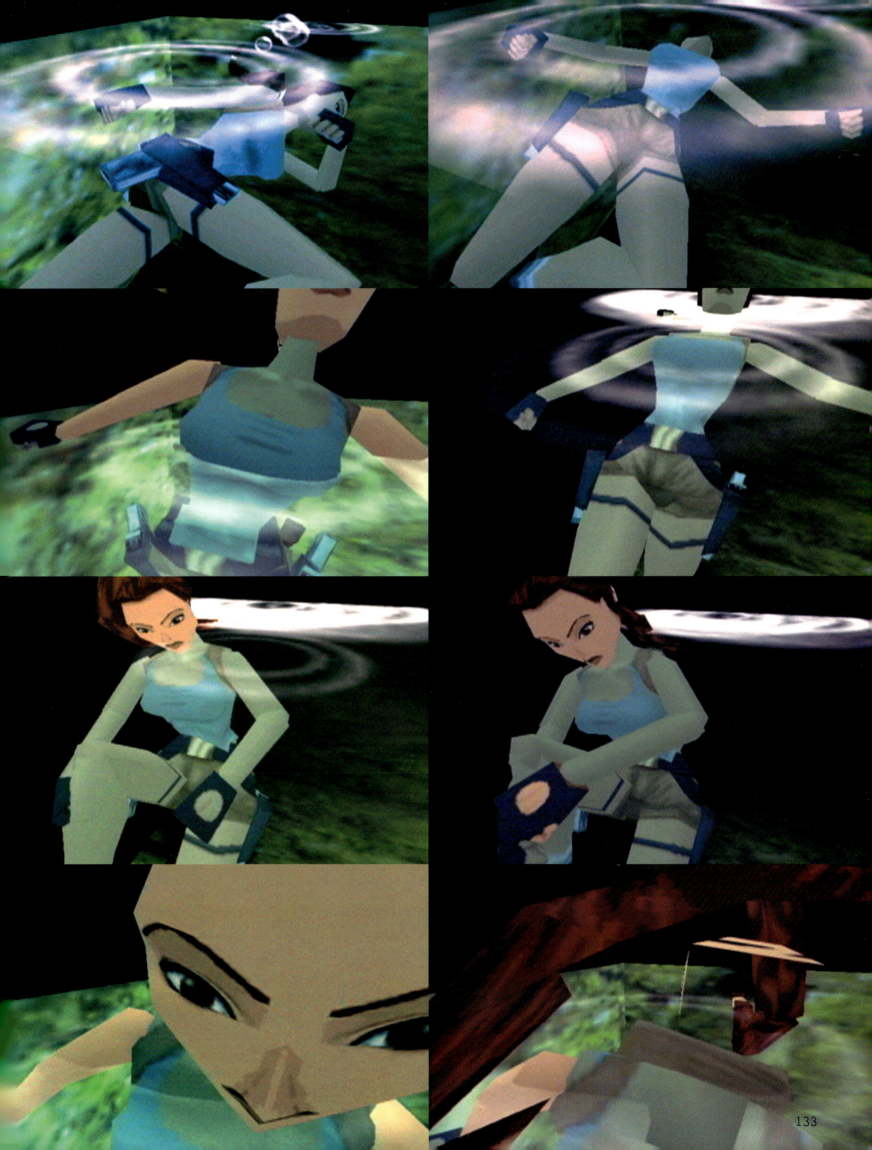

133

134

135

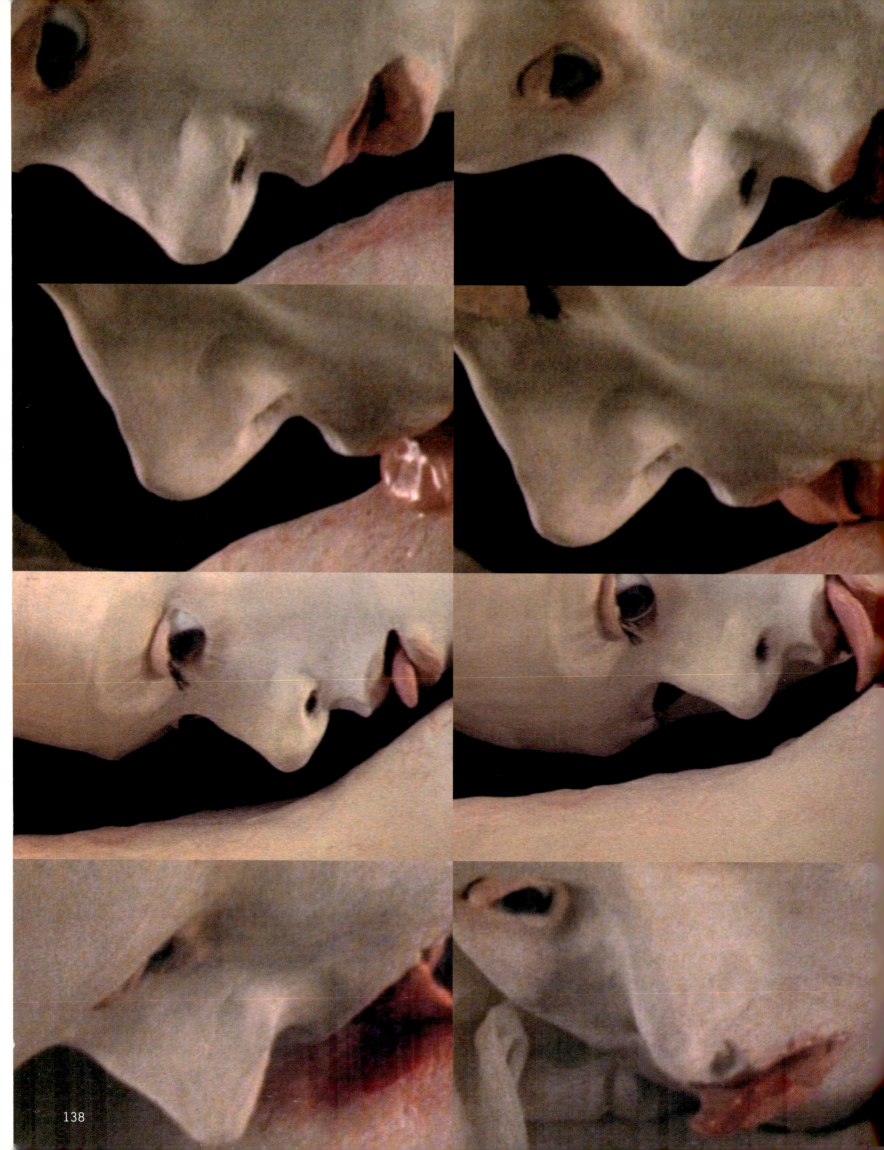

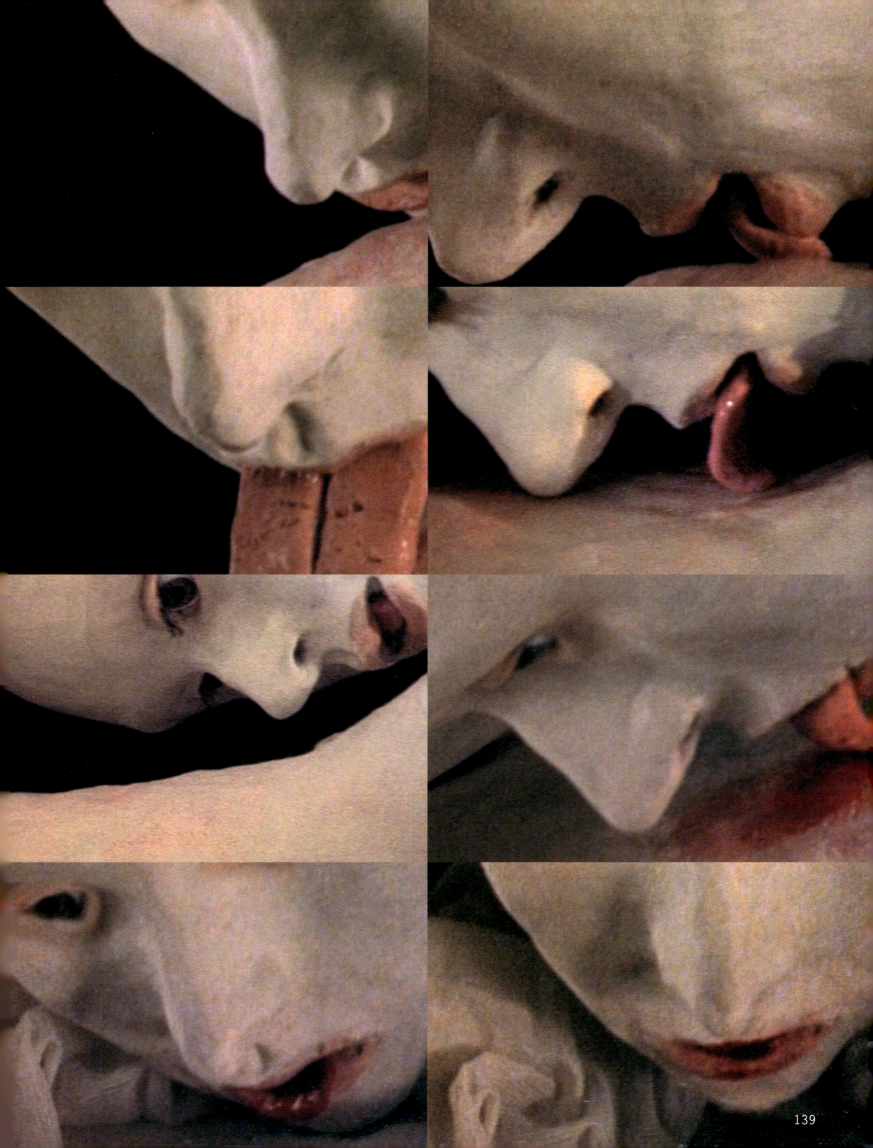

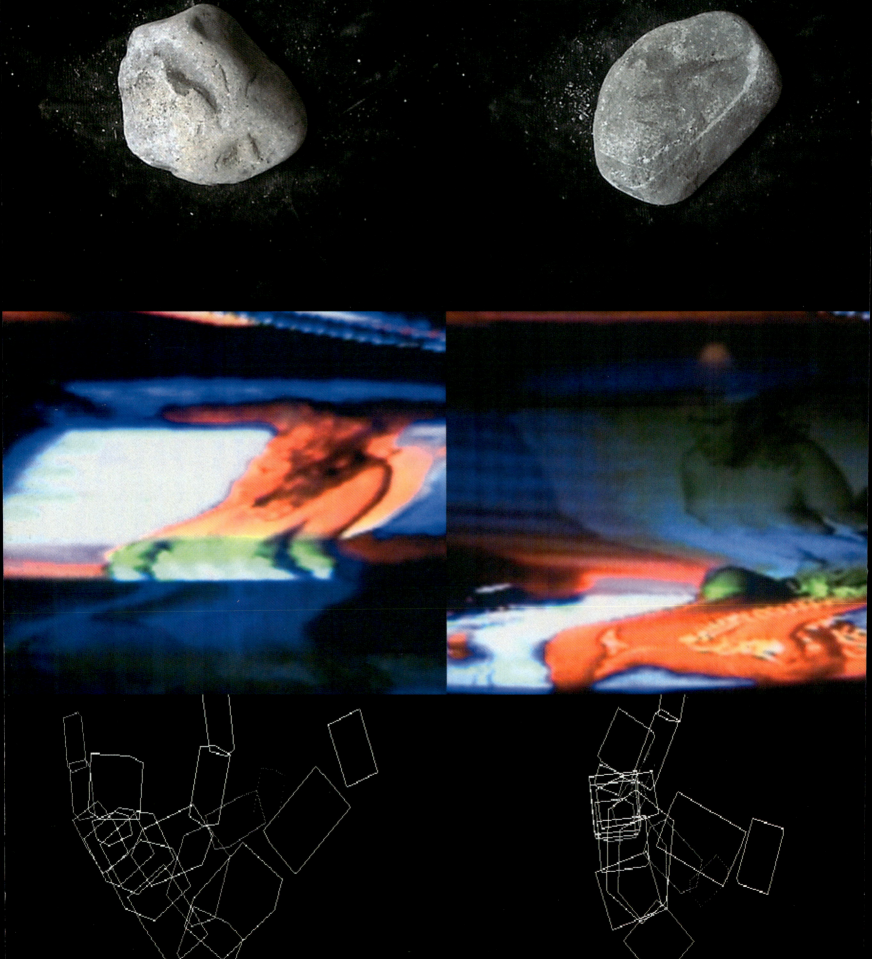

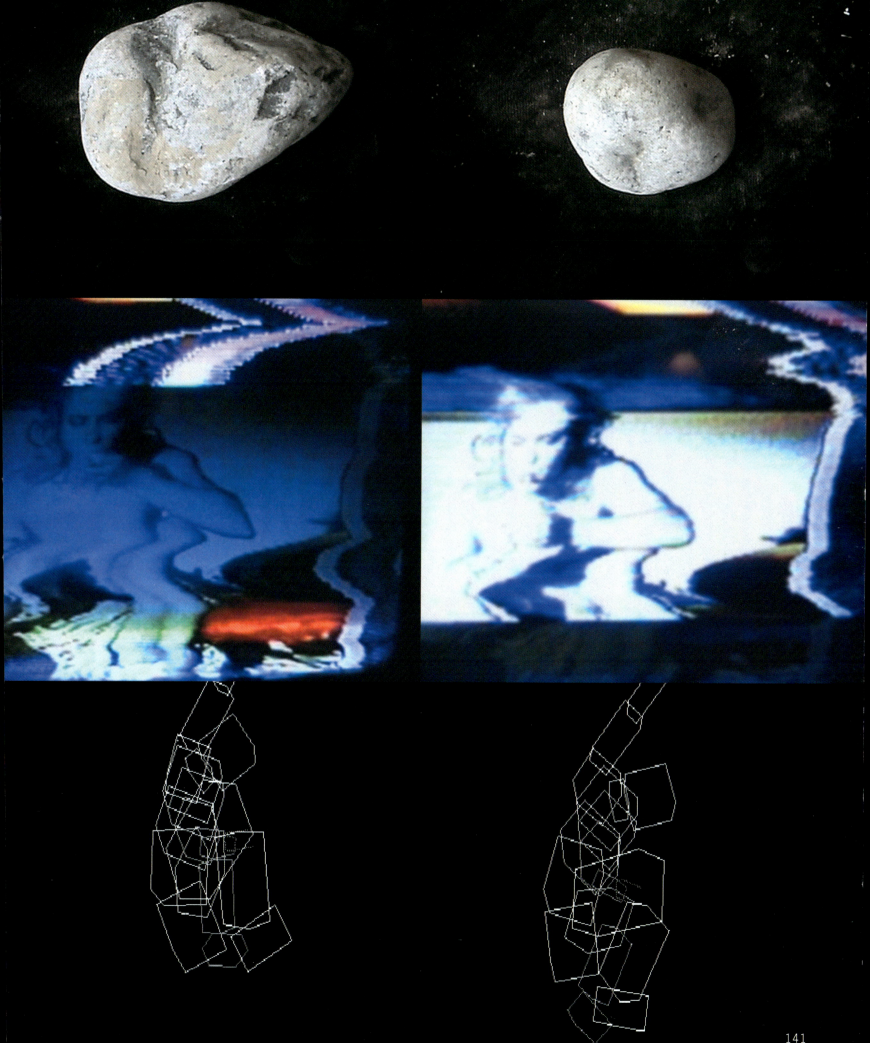

Claudia Hart
Teresa Seemann
David Galbraith
Jennifer and Kevin McCoy

every anvil, every airplane, every baseball bat, every big hammer, every bomb, every box or package, eve
every falling object, every fire, every gun, every grenade, every hatchet, every hole, every jet pack, every
stick, every suitcase, every tombstone, every train, every trap, every white flag, every adrift at sea, every
and scratching, every climbing, every clothes coming off, every cooking a character, every crashing, every
escape, every fall from a great height, every fighting, every force feeding, every gigantic step, every settii
hat over face, every pulling, every pounding, every poking, every poisoning, every pie in face, every mimicl
down, every jumping on head, every hunting, every hitting on head, every hiding, every hanging by a threac
and fall, every smash over head, every sneaking, every spanking, every spinning, every spitting, every spra
stop, every strangling, every suicide, every sword fight, every thinking and planning, every throwing, eve
whistle, every insult, every growl, every death wish, every cry, every cough, every laugh, every moan, ev
every falling apart, every fight cloud, every flattened character, every speed cloud, every tornado spin, eve
and lust, every moment of realization, every panic, every post-traumatic condition, every profuse sw
unconsciousness, every dumb character, every deception, every disguise, every costume, every evil genius, e

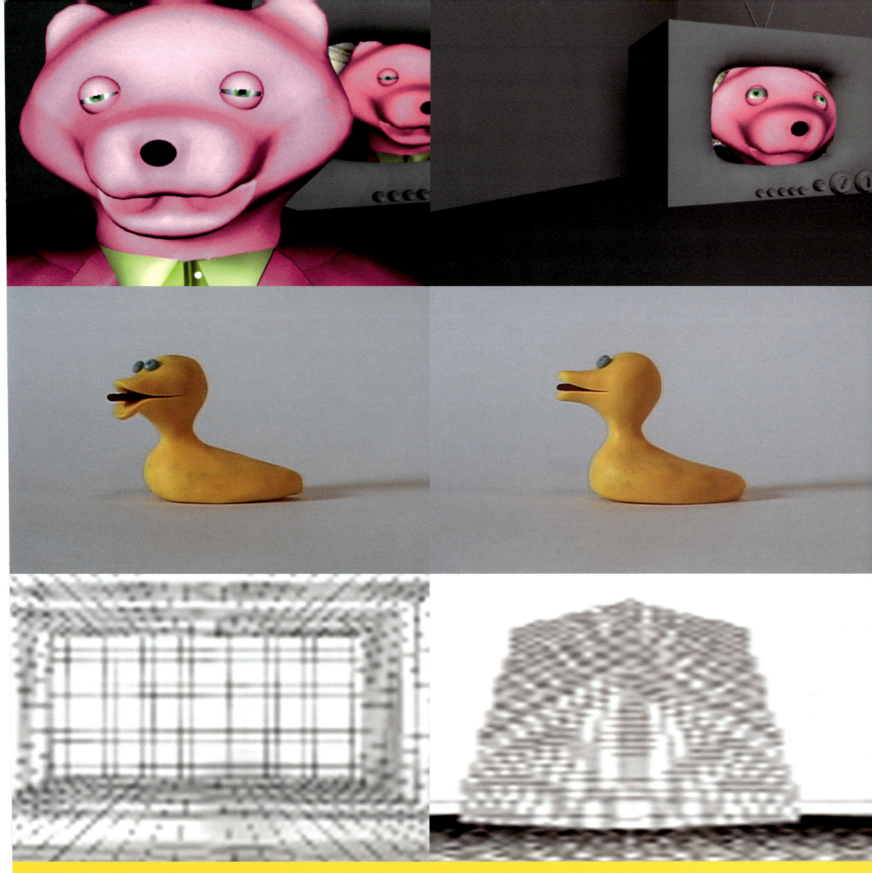

every cliff, every cigar and cigarette, every decoy, every dynamite, every exploding cigar, every fake hole, very machine and contraption, every mousetrap, every rocket, every shovel, every sign, every siren, every very biting, every breaking things, every burial, every capture, every careening, every chase, every clawing g through, every dancing, every digging, every diving, every eating a character, every fall down stairs, every every running really fast, every running into something, every running away, every punching, every pulling y lying in wait, every looking around, every kiss, every kicking, every kick in the ass, every jumping up and grimacing, every grabbing, every shaking, every shooting, every slamming a door, every slapping, every slip ater, every staggering, every stalking a victim, every stealing clothes, every stepping off cliff, every sudden g, every whacking, every bad singing, every barking, every beg and plead, every brrr/yei yei, every call or am, every threat, every yell, every bubbles, every distorted body, every cloud of smoke, every explosion, g odor, every visualized sound, every ailment, every death, every fear, every guilt, every hunger, every love very seeing stars or hearts, every singed fur or hair, every tied in knots, every turning colors, every le, every ferocious animal, every headless character, every hunter, every mean dog, every monster, every thug

145

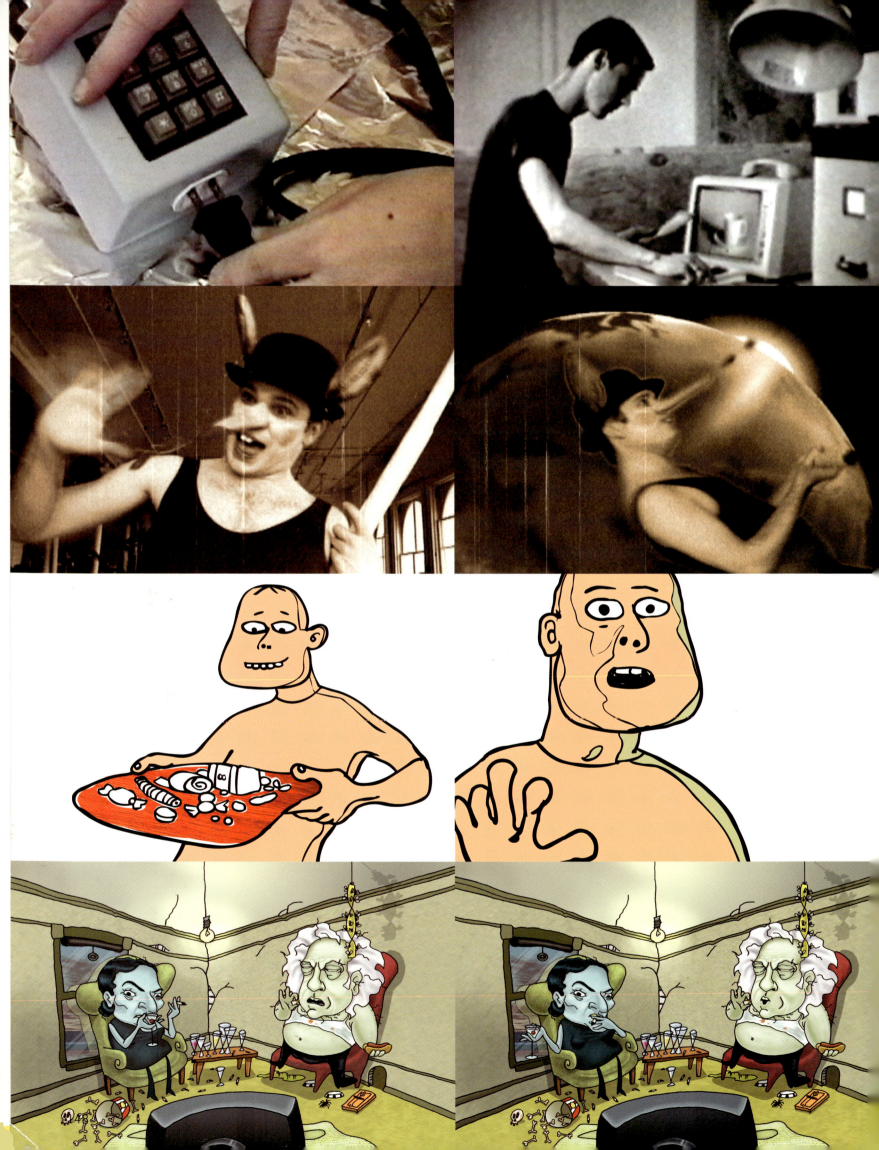

ON THE WEB
Environment designed by Paul Johnson

John Klima
Eric Zimmerman and Word.com
Mark Napier
Andy Deck
JODI
Mark Daggett
Natalie Bookchin
Golan Levin and Casey Reas
Mouchette
Panajotis Mihalatos
Joshua Davis
Xeth Feinberg
Alex and Munro Galloway
Sebastian Luetgert
YOUNG HAE CHANG HEAVY INDUSTRIES

(152) Top to bottom: installation view, web animation room, P.S.1 Contemporary Art Center, 2001,
photo courtesy Eileen Costa; Paul Johnson,
Binocular Projector, 1995
Hoover Wet and Dry, 2001

(153) Top to bottom: John Klima, *Glasbead*, 2000,
www.glasbead.com, *SiSSYFiGHT 2000*, 2000, www.sis-
syfight.com
P-Soup, 2000, www.potatoland.org/p-soup
Open Studio, 2001, www.artcontext.org/draw
JODI, *ASDFG*, 1999, asdfg.jodi.org

(154) Top to bottom: Mark Daggett, *Blur Browser*,
2001, www.flavoredthunder.com/dev/browser-ges-
tures
Natalie Bookchin, *The Intruder*, 1999,
www.calarts.edu/~bookchin/intruder
Golan Levin and Casey Reas, *Dakadaka*, 2000,
acg.media.mit.edu/projects/dakadaka/dakadaka.html
Mouchette, *Lullaby for a Dead Fly*, 2000,
www.mouchette.org/fly
Panajotis Mihalatos, *Flexible Planning*, 2000,
users.otenet.gr/~pan_mi/drclb.htm

(155): Joshua Davis, *Machine # 09182001*, 2001,
www.praystation.com
Xeth Feinberg, *Bulbo in the 20th Century*, 2000,
www.bulbo.com, www.bulbo.com/bmovies/bulbo-
20th.html
Sebastian Luetgert, *The Coils of the Serpent part
1*, 1999–2001, rolux.org/index.php3
Alex and Munro Galloway, *Day In, Day Out*, 2001,
networked software application
YOUNG-HAE CHANG HEAVY INDUSTRIES, *DAKOTA*, 2001,
www.yhchang.com/dakota.html

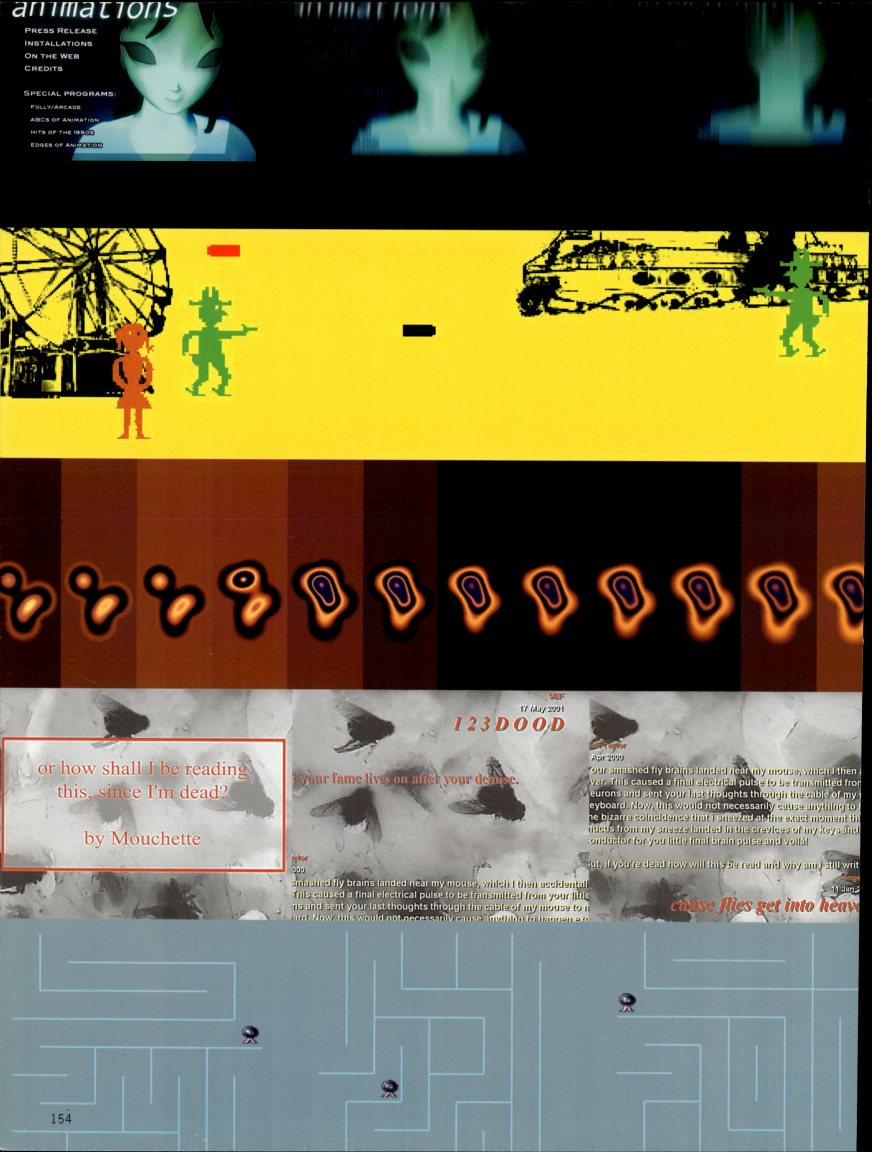

SØ GØD DAMN
T ALL,

WHY THE
HELL

DØES ELIE

APPEAR,

155

FOLLY
Environment designed by John Pilson and Andrea Mason

J. Tobias Andersson
Avish Khebrehzadch
Ingrid Bromberg
Sarah Ciraci
Maureen Connor
Melanie Crean
Deborah Davidovitz
Rory Hanrahan
Tim Hirzel
Xana Kudriacev-DeMilner
Omar Lewis and Jason Cooper
Daniel Lefcourt
Cecilia Lundquist
Joe McKay
Rupert Norfolk
Diego Perrone
Root R (Shingo Suzuki)
Jonathan Rosen
Kathy Rose
Jason Schiedel
Matthew Suib
Scott Teplin
Florian Zeyfang

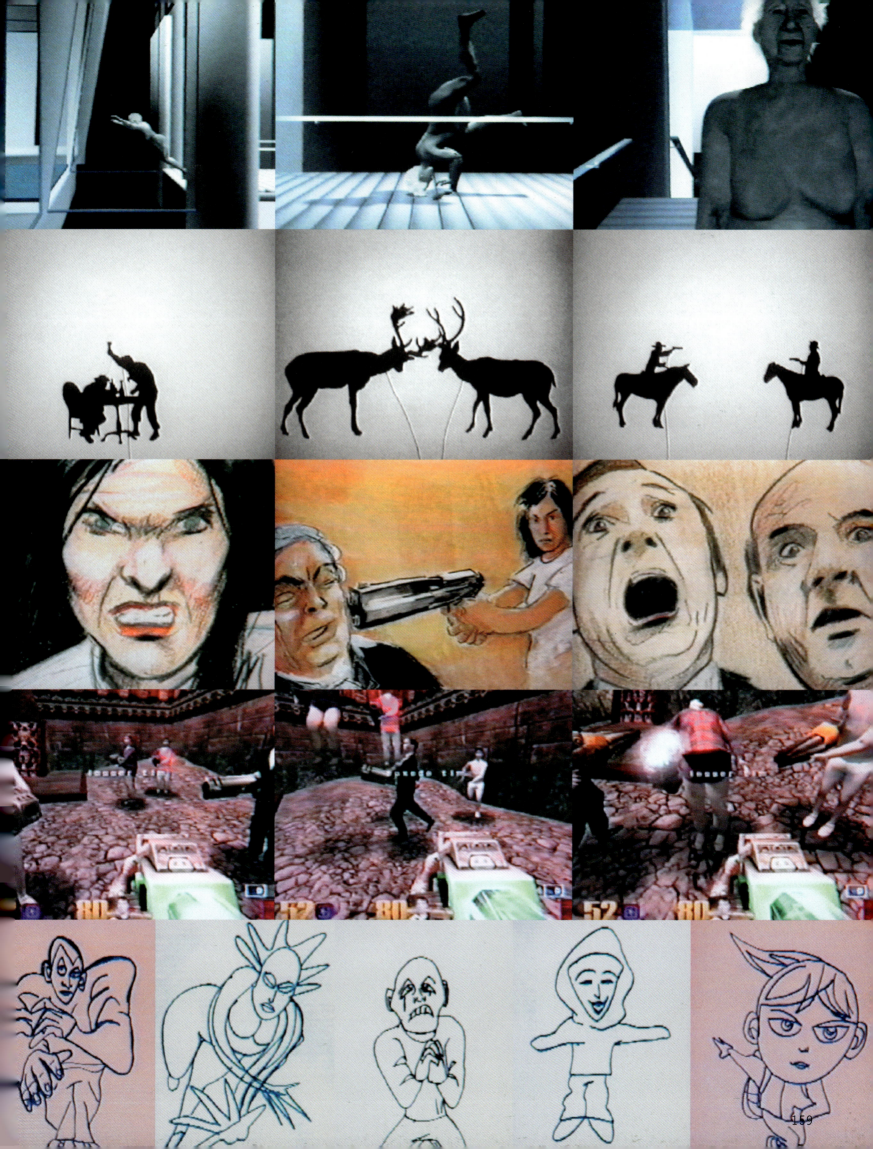

159

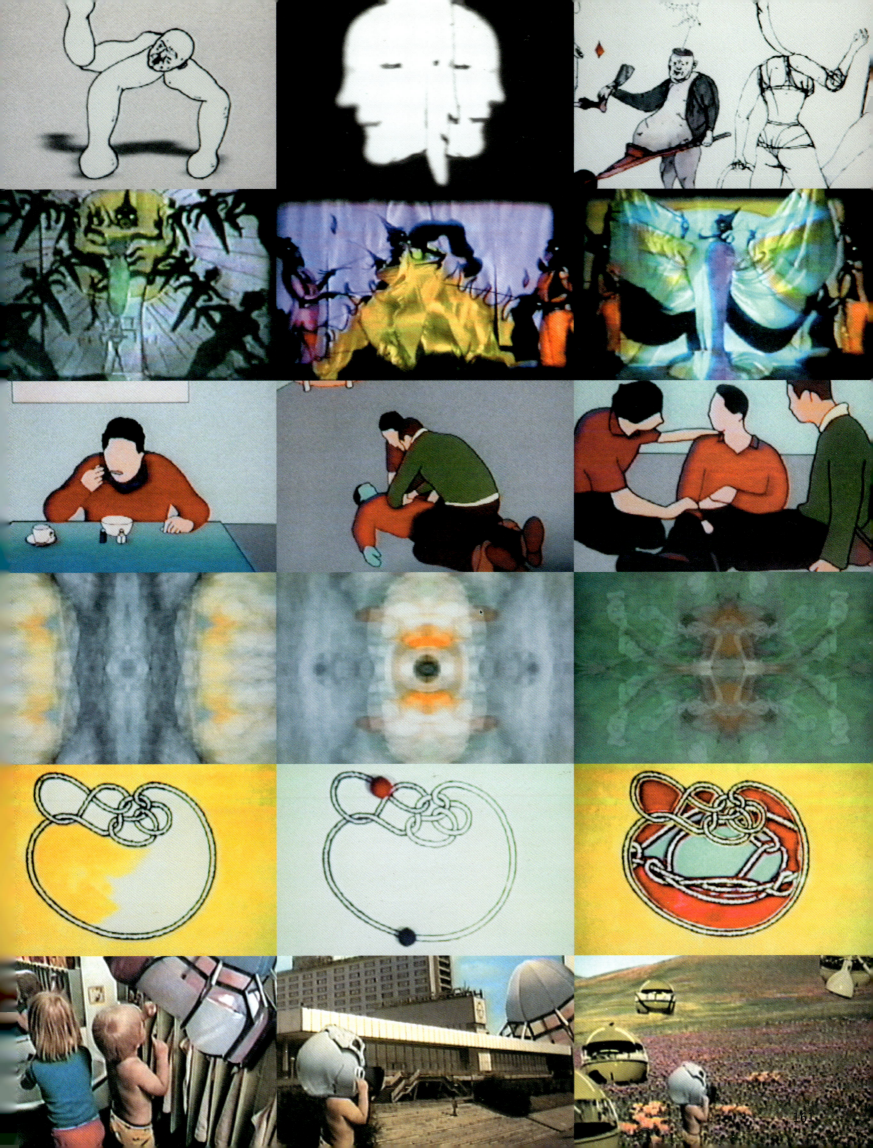

Artists' Statements
and Biographies

PEGGY AHWESH

*Like earlier magical entertainments that generated new ways of expressing the body technological, such as the Automata or the late 19th century trick film (magicians transforming women into butterflies, skeletons or angels, etc),
Lara Croft is the girl-doll of the late 20th century gaming world. What we like most about her is that she is a collection of cones and cylinders — not a human at all — most worthy as a repository for our post-feminist fantasies of adventure, sex and violence without consequence. But what we fall back on is that she is almost human. The limited inventory of her gestures and the militaristic rigor of the game strategies created for her by the programmers is a repetition compulsion of sorts, offering some kind of cyberagency and cyberprowess for the player. As I played the game, I recorded it live onto tape, collecting hours of footage. Then I re-edited the material "found footage." Ignoring the original drive of the action, I make Lara a vehicle for my thoughts on what I see as the triad of her personas: the alien, the orphan and the clone. Quotations are from* The Book of Disquiet *by Fernando Pessoa,* The Female Man *by Joanna Russ and jazz mystic Sun Ra.*

Peggy Ahwesh came of age in the 1970's with feminism and the punk underground. She works in film and digital media, making experimental work about the fantasies, identities and desires of the woman subject. Ahwesh was the subject of a mid-career retrospective at the Whitney Museum of American Art in 1997. Other retrospectives: Filmmuseum, Brussels; The Carpenter Center at Harvard University, Cambridge, MA and Anthology Film Archives, New York. Ahwesh has shown at the Flaherty Film Seminar, The Jerusalem Cinematheque, The Pompidou Center in Paris, The New York Film Festival and the 1991, 1995 and 2002 Biennials at the Whitney Museum of American Art, New York among others. Ahwesh is a member of the editorial committee of the book publishing collective Ediciones la Calavera. She teaches film and video production at Bard College, Annandale, NY. Her audio collaboration with Barbara Ess (Y Pants, UltraVulva) was recently released on the Ecstatic Peace label. Currently, Ahwesh is collaborating with Bobby Abate on *Certain Women*, a feature length melodrama.

HALUK AKAKÇE

This project is about the complexity of relations. Two elements act and react upon each other: an interplay in dialexia. Two lives, two ideas, integrated to a degree that they define and give birth to each other. The piece explores the relationship between an "element of nature" and "the nature of an element". The relation between them is not about combination, but rather a folding of identity and autonomy. Glow-in-the-dark threads make a space embracing all to be one and two, so luminous caring and a duel of elements fills you up and nourish like life forest. A series of random configurations comes alive as they multiply and separate. Their changes occur in a field of contexuality losing their individual signification unveiling a tenuous evolution of their interplay and creating infinite identities.

Haluk Akakçe was born in 1970, in Ankara, Turkey and lives in New York. Solo presentations of his work have been seen at the Whitney Museum at Phillip Morris, New York (2002), Centro Nazional per lei Arti Contemporanee, Rome (2002) at Centre d'Art Contemporain, Geneva (2001), Deitch Projects, New York (2001), Henry Urbach Architecture, New York (2000) and P.S.1 Contemporary Art Center, New York (2000). His work has been included in group shows at Shanghai Biennial and Bienal de Sao Paulo (2002), the Walker Art Center, Minneapolis, MN (2001), Casino/Luxembourg Forum d'Art Contemporain (2000), the Istanbul Biennial (1999), and the Drawing Center, New York (1998).

FRANCIS ALŸS

*A small video projector faces the wall, sitting on a wooden chair.
On the wall, the image of a woman endlessly pours water from one glass to another.
Next to her, on a small table, a record player which has been set on auto-replay melancholically sings:
"Mañana, Mañana is soon enough for me."*

Francis Alÿs was born in Antwerp, Belgium, in 1959. After studying architecture in Europe he traveled to Mexico in 1987 to work as an architect. He divides his time between Mexico City, New York and London. Solo presentations of his work have been seen at The Museum of Modern Art, New York and the Castello di Rivoli, Turin (2002), the Wadsworth Athenaeum, Hartford, CT (2001), Galerie de l'UQAM, Montreal (2000), and the Lisson Gallery, London (2001, 1999). He has been included in group exhibitions: the 2002 Lima Biennale, Lima; at P.S.1 Contemporary Art Center and Kunst-Werke Berlin (2002); the 7th Istanbul Biennial, Istanbul; Venice Biennale, Venice (1999); and Walker Art Center, Minneapolis, MN (all 2001), among many others.

OLADÉLÉ AJIBOYÉ BAMGBOYÉ

Notions of the encounter remain prominent in my artwork. The responsibility that we have towards the Other, is equally crucial and how these are negotiated within the constructed architecture of the exhibition space is a prime concern within the conceptualization, execution of my work.
Body was conceived in the present form for "Dire Aids: Say Aids" and explores the issues of secrecy, intimacy, the performative and a benign sense of place. It centers on the encounter with the body of the Other, at once accessible through technology, but always to remain distant. Manipulating imagery from various popular live-on-demand sources that dislocate the body, the work explores the nature of the secrecy of the heterosexual myth that AIDS is nevertheless a homosexual condition.
In many parts of Britain for example, many youths participate in the risk of unprotected and casual sex, often thinking that they are beyond the AIDS epidemic. After all, how could it affect them? My aim in the work is to subvert that very element of secrecy that implores perversion, that encourages the excitement of risk taking.
We can have everything and everyone on demand, and wherever we choose. The work however focuses on the nature of fragility, about the dangers of extra-persona projection onto the Other. In this sense the Other is defined as that which can be bought, tamed and submitted to a will.
The work will use the video projection in the gallery, manipulated through computer animation and digital techniques, clarifies and draws our attention to the individual frames that may be missed in the actual installation. In this way our myth of subsuming time is realized.
The anonymous soundtrack, despite its often

haunting nature, offers the audience some necessary respite from the increasingly intense imagery. It is also for this reason that the projection is carried out in a room that is not painted black in the traditional video projection sense. In fact, if the viewer is perceptive he/she is able to discern the faint image of a room lamp that is prominent in the projected image. In this way, the viewer is encouraged to consider this installation as a replica of a living environment and it is then that the imagery of the work transcends the mere reworking of found imagery into something more spiritual. It also seeks to avoid the dramatic or the tragic. While the work deals, naturally, with the very serious matter of AIDS, it is not ultimately about it. It seeks to question at personal level the apparent dislocation of the self from the body, and the associated unsettling effects, brought on by communication technology. The work maintains that it is perhaps the breakdown or even lack of communication between people that continues to propagate the AIDS epidemic globally. Finally while an artwork cannot and may not even seek to preach or desire to alter societal habits, one of its endearing strengths continues to be that of focusing the attention of the viewers of the work on an issue of great importance. Like the majority of my work, Body also begins to operate in the realm of the post-exhibition experience on the encounter of the work.

Oladélé Bamgboyé was born 1963, in Odo-Eku, Nigeria. Solo presentations of his work have been seen at the Witte de With Center for Contemporary Art, Rotterdam (2000), the Thomas Erben Gallery, New York (2002, 2000) and ArtPace in San Antonio, Texas (1999). His work has been included in exhibitions at the Reina Sofia, Madrid, Spain (2002), the Borusan Art Gallery, Istanbul, Turkey, the Museum Villa Stuck, Munich, the Museum of Contemporary Art, Chicago, and P.S.1 Contemporary Art Center, New York (all 2001/2002); Bildmuseet, Ume' Universitet, Sweden; the Tate Britain, London, and the Museé d'Art Moderne de la Ville de Paris (all 2000). Bamgboyé participated the 2002 Taipei Biennale, the Triennale of Contemporary Art, Yokohama (2001), and Documenta X, Kassel (1997).

JEREMY BLAKE

Guccinam *depicts dreamlike states using a combination of architectural and abstract imagery. I refer to this work as "time-based painting," and employ a painterly sensibility and process to create images that transform over time. Guccinam isn't meant to evoke any issue directly related to the Vietnam War, nor is it meant to recall any actual place. My noticing some relatively vague traces of both martial and colonial aesthetics in contemporary design inspired the imagery in the piece. Examples range from the bamboo handles on expensive Gucci purses and silverware, to the battle-ready appearance of sport utility vehicles, to the camouflage gear sported by countless urban hipsters. I was also interested in making a piece that employed some of the same brightly tinted smoke and droning mechanical noise that are standard elements in Hollywood films that deal with the war in Vietnam. I particularly admired the painterly use of tinted smoke in* Apocalypse Now. Guccinam *is best understood as an attempt to build a hallucinatory location where a perceived strain in popular aesthetics is deliberately intensified.*

Jeremy Blake was born in 1971, at Ft Sill, Oklahoma. A solo exhibition is planned at the Museo Nacional Centro de Arte Reina Sofia, Madrid, Spain (2003). Other solo exhibitions have taken place at the Museum of Contemporary Art, San Diego, San Diego, CA, and Galerie Ghislaine Hussenot, Paris (2002), Art Basel 2000, Basel; Works on Paper, Inc., Los Angeles (2001, 1999) and Feigen Contemporary, New York (2000, 1999). Blake's work has been included in group exhibitions at the San Francisco Museum of Modern Art, San Francisco, CA; the Whitney Museum of American Art, New York, (both 2001), P.S.1 Contemporary Art Center, New York, and Centre Georges Pompidou, Paris (both 2000), and the Institute for Contemporary Art, London (1999). Blake participated in the Whitney Biennial at the Whitney Museum of American Art, New York in 2000 and 2002.

ANGUS FAIRHURST

Short seamless loops of action: self-perpetuating, isolated, stubborn, never-ending; self-defeating, continually self-creating; almost faltering, unable to complete the cycle, but miraculously inevitably doing so; following an outside imperative (the time structure); driven by its own necessity to complete, to finish, in order to be able to start. This manipulation, the short circuit, is possible in animation. It also affords opportunities to simplify and to complicate: to strip down figures to a bare minimum, a set of lines, then by overlaying sequences out of sync (out of time), to break down the fluency of those lines, that representation. The breakdown can continue until nothing remains of what you started with, and what you have now is maybe more than you wanted. An overload of sequences out of time. The proper things don't have their boundaries any more. Individual elements no longer perform according to their prescribed sphere; metaphors are no longer fixed between either this or that, but are mushed together, the lines are broken-up, crossed-over, undone. They interfere with each other, and with themselves. To get back to the beginning is now further.

The structure of Normal/Distorted/Superimposed: *a circle, turning at one revolution every sixty seconds, is made up of twelve separate elements each performing its own interior function, some smoothly, some unevenly. These elements are overlapped upon themselves in progressive layers, each layer at a different stage in the time sequence. The out-of-sync becomes the in-sync, what is independent becomes interdependent. As it breaks down it builds up. The intrinsic function of each element no longer has any overall relevance. It seems destructive at first but then there appears a different type of image. The black lily is over-gilded, the circle becomes dense. Each individual element is sticking tenaciously to its task, but it becomes apparent that new tasks are needed as the old ones die. The something "new" is not something that hasn't been seen in some way or other, in some place or other, but new in terms of the breakdown.*

Angus Fairhurst was born in 1966 in Kent, England, and lives and works in London. Solo exhibitions of his work have been presented at the Alphadelta Gallery — Artio Gallery, Athens, (2002), Kunsthalle St. Gallen (1999), the Kölnischer Kunstverein, Cologne (1998) and the Anton Kern Gallery, New York (1998). He has par-

ticipated in group shows at the ZKM Center for
Media Art and Technology, Karlsruhe (2000), the
Kunsthalle Vienna (1998) and the Contemporary Art
Museum, Houston, TX (1995).

DAVID GALBRAITH
*Start with an icon of hyper-linear culture: the
3D, perspectival, architectonic design grid.
Subject it to a simple procedure, using basic
modeling operations to produce an emergent phenomenon; namely, deploy scale shift and projection in time to create individual images
(frames), then sequence these, obtaining an animation. Adopt a one-take aesthetic. Choose figure
over line, and embrace holes, displacements,
gaps, ephemera. Instead of a proper place, create
a shifting site.*

David Galbraith was born in 1965, in Milwaukee,
WI and lives and works in New York. His work has
been included in group exhibitions at P.S.1
Contemporary Art Center, New York, among others.
Two-person shows with his collaborative partner
Teresa Seemann have been seen at The New Museum
of Contemporary Art, New York and the Soap
Factory, Minneapolis, MN (both 2001). His music
performance project — *The Experimental Makeup*, an
electronic duo with artist/musician Michael J.
Mahalchick — has performed extensively since 1999
with dates in Munich, Los Angeles and New York.

LIAM GILLICK
*(lipsync) [exhale]
(lipsync) [tut]
(voice-over) This is a revised construction.
Something that can only be described. I have
negotiated every step of the way. Taking tiny
steps. Every move through this place is turning.
Functioning in space idea.
(lipsync) [uh......] (voice-over) This garden is
a product of my thought, my one thought, my many
thoughts. My thoughts and projections are constructions.
(lipsync) [bum bum bummmmmm]
(voice-over) I shifted and some things moved with
me and were dragged around. From one place to
another up down and up down. Descriptions of
rumour. There was another place just like this.
There was another place in colour. Two came there
with some simple furniture.*

*(lipsync) [exhale]
(voice-over) They smiled and nodded and I remember them working fast. Later we all danced on
things. Stomping down hard and fast.
(lipsync) [breath in deeply]
(woman's voice) I was not there to see it all as
I had not been constructed yet. My thoughts and
projections are applied. Some pass me by. But I
you propose a new identity. Never openly, only
through others.
(voice-over) I've got some instructions for me
and you. People pass me by, catching images and
locations.
(lipsync) [breathe out hard through nose [snort]]
(voice-over) Most of the time things work well.
Things work well without presence but I will try
to propose what I have seen.
(voice-over) There is a place on the other side
of the world. Somewhere in the south there is the
last big island. When it rains, it really rains.
It was nearly destroyed, but the clouds were too
low. And still cry.
(voice-over) [hmmm hmmm ba hmmm bum]
(voice-over) How long should I sit? Storing
ideas.
(voice-over) This is semi-public. I you propose
some pictures from another place. There were
lumps and forms, which I try to describe.
(voice-over) Some things arrived when I too was
constructed. I arrived in time to leak constructions from questions. Semi-private becomes semi-
public.
(lipsync) [tut] (voice-over) I you propose some
changes. Keep shifting from side to side. A projection from another place is required here, not
the projection of an image, but a projection of
settled thinking.
(lipsync) [ha]*

Liam Gillick was born in 1964, in Aylesbury,
England, and lives and works in New York and
London. Solo exhibitions have been organized at
Museum of Modern Art, New York (2003); Schipper
und Krome/Max Hetzler, Berlin (2003, 2000); Casey
Kaplan 10—6, New York (2003, 2001), The
Whitechapel Art Gallery, London and Palais de
Tokyo, Paris (2002); Tate Britain, London (2001);
CCA Kitakyushu, Tokyo and Hayward Gallery, London
(2000). His work has been included in group exhi-
bitions at Tate Britain, London (2002); Moderna

Museet, Stockholm (2001); The Approach, London (1998), and many others.

CLAUDIA HART

The presentation format for this work was intended to be a large TV, placed on the floor in the corner of a dark room, mirroring the scene represented in the animation: a TV in the corner of a dark room, broadcasting a "talking head" — a stuffed bear, speaking in a corner of a dark room standing in front of a TV in a corner of a dark room, also broadcasting the same talking head — a stuffed bear, speaking in a corner of a dark room... ad infinitum. More Life is a recursive system — meaning a self reflecting system — one which uses itself to build itself — just like those used in the programming languages of thinking machines like the computer.

The sound track is a grab from the 1982 Ridley Scott film Blade Runner, in which Roy Batty, the renegade replicant played by Rutger Hauer, explains to his creator, the founder of the Tyrell Corporation, why he is about to kill him. "I want more life, fucker," is what Roy Batty demands of Tyrell, reproaching him bitterly because Tyrell has programmed all of the androids produced by his corporation to have only a limited two year life span. "I want more life, fucker," Batty growls, right before he crushes Tyrell's head.

The piece is intended to be both a tragic and an ironic comment on the virtual world generally and specifically, the world of the imaginary, which is animation itself.

After graduating from Columbia University School of Architecture, Claudia Hart began her professional life as a critic, serving as Reviews Editor for *Artforum* and Associate Editor of *ID: the Magazine of International Design*. Her early work consisted of paintings of book pages, which she also wrote, and showed with the Pat Hearn Gallery, New York. After receiving a National Endowment for the Arts Visual Arts Fellowship in 1989, she shifted her practice to Europe, showing with Tanit Gallery in Cologne and Munich. After receiving an American Center fellowship in Paris, Hart moved ultimately to Berlin after receiving a Künstlerhaus Bethanien grant. In Berlin, she received numerous foundation and government grants, including the Frauen Stipendium from the Berlin Senate, the Luftbrückendank Foundation Grant, the Berlin Kulturfond and the federal Kunstfond Bonn with the curator Katrin Becker, and presented projects with Kunst-Werke, NGBK, Galerie Wohnmachine, Shift Kunstverein, and NBK among others. Hart returned to New York in 1998, and has since published two illustrated books, *A Child's Machiavelli*, and *Night Fears*. In 2001, she received a degree from New York University's Center for Advanced Digital Applications in Computer Animation. At present, she teaches at Pratt Institute and shows her work with Sandra Gering Gallery, New York.

SIMON HENWOOD

For me, traditional cell and stop-motion animation has always been about making the physically impossible believable. Dinosaurs, talking mice, or whatever one can imagine. Now, CG animation is striving to copy reality by making a perfect computer generated human being. This obsession to make an accurate copy of nature is a major driving force in software development. The application of a truly successful result would certainly justify the scale of investment. CG's other potentials (with only a handful of truly outstanding exceptions) have only been explored in advertising or the effects film industry. The results generally date very quickly and are mostly unimaginative and devoid of an individual touch.

The major theme of my work is childhood. I have always loved cartoons and Johnny Pumpkin is about making a cartoon in that tradition without the usual constraints of a broadcaster's slot. It's also about respecting the traditions of the medium while making full use of the technology at the time.

With animation, one has to be completely committed to the whole process to gain a result. Initially, I liked the idea of developing 2D drawings into their CG counterparts, and then seeing them come alive. After I got over this stage, I found that the real challenge was about the strength to make choices. The decisions involved are nothing like any other medium I have worked in as an artist. To keep the individual vision meant that I had to continually learn processes and new languages just to effectively

communicate with the animators. Though I have
directed film and made traditional animations in
the past, CG practically demands a commitment to
the very air the characters breathe.
Good character animation, like a good comic, only
ever works if you apply real attention to every
aspect of structure and detail. Maintaining this
without losing the spontaneity of the idea is the
challenge. Making it look easy is in the mastering, and mastering it is a life long commitment.

Simon Henwood was born in 1965, in Portsmouth,
England. He has presented his work at the UCLA
Hammer Museum, Los Angeles (2000–01), at Asprey
Jacques, London and the Richard Heller Gallery,
Santa Monica (2000) and ICA, London (1999). He
has created and illustrated several magazines and
children's books.

PIERRE HUYGHE
I can imagine you… it's easy!
I can see you… and I can see her!
I am looking at an image! Facing an imaginary
character.
She is a passer-by, an extra, she was designed
just like that.
Nobody planned that she would ever have to
speak.
Given no particular ability to survive, she would
probably be dead by now.
This is her true story: a fictional character with a
copyright designed by a company and proposed for
sale. That's it…
While waiting to be dropped into a story, she has
been diverted from a
fictional existence and has become, what she is
now, a deviant sign…
She says
I've got two minutes, two minutes of your linear
time.
That's more than what I would have spent anyway
in a story before being
forgotten…in less than two minutes I'll be gone.
My name, my name is Annlee, Annlee, I've a common
name,
I was a frozen picture, an evidence submitted to
you.
I have become animated however not by a story
with a plot,
no… I'm haunted by your imagination… and that's

what I want from you…
See, I'm not here for your amusement… You are
here for mine!
… it was pretty… (hum)…
(little girl)… it was pretty neat, all the paintings
were really nice but I saw
one, this one painting really caught my eye, it was
called "waterlilies," I look
at it and I gaze at it, and then I look at the
painting next to it, it really was
astonishing, and I forgot everything else that I've
ever known, I couldn't even
look at the name of the painting, all I saw was the
girl in the boat
I look at her, I wonder what she was thinking, I
don't know, maybe she was
Suffering, maybe she was hurting…
I look at it, I look at it
I couldn't think, I couldn't breathe…
I don't know what happened
I was stuck…
… I saw a strange light
I didn't know what it was, then I felt a beam on my
shoulder
I feel something stronger on my shoulder
It hit me, it hit me, it hurt and finally, I saw
the light
and it was getting bigger
and bigger and bigger until I could see nothing
else
Finally I felt nothing, I was gone!

Pierre Huyghe was born in 1962 in Paris, where he
currently lives and works. His work has been presented in numerous solo exhibitions including
shows at the Kunsthaus Bregenz, Bregenz, Austria
(2002); Musée d' Art Moderne et Contemporain,
Geneva (2001); the Stedelijk Van Abbemuseum,
Amsterdam (2001); Musée d'Art Contemporain,
Montreal (2000–2001); Centre Georges Pompidou,
Paris; the Renaissance Society, University of
Chicago and the Museum of Contemporary Art,
Chicago (2000); Aarhus Kunstmuseum, Denmark
(1999); and the Musée d'Art Moderne de la Ville
de Paris (1998). His work has been represented in
group exhibitions at the Solomon R. Guggenheim
Museum, New York (2003); the Kunsthalle Zürich;
Institute for Visual Culture, Cambridge; and
SFMoMA, San Francisco, CA (2002); The Hirshhorn
Museum, Washington D.C., and Haus der Kunst,

Munich (1999–2000); and the Guggenheim Museum SoHo, New York (1998). He participated in the Documenta 11, Kassel (2002); Istanbul Biennial (1999); the Carnegie International, Pittsburgh (1999); the Venice Biennale (1999 and 2001); and the second Johannesburg Biennial (1997). Huyghe received the 2002 Hugo Boss Prize.

PAUL JOHNSON

I am showing a cross-section of projectors and gaming devices I've built since 1995. There are also several browsers to view web content by other artists. My first projectors have a rough look to them. The videos are of large commercial spaces shot so they appeared a little like documentary footage. The collapsed, snow covered stadium projected by the Binocular Projector looks a little like war footage. Monocular Projector depicts perpetual freefall into a bottomless hotel lobby.

The work became smaller and compact over time. I began building flashlight projectors because I wanted people to have an intimate experience of the work. There is a lot of fine detail in these pieces and it is not unusual for people to get down on their hands and knees to view the work. The videos evolved from documentary-like to pure computer animation. I eventually wound up building computers instead of projectors... although I still build projectors.

I try to work with the complete technology; not just the image. The work does not culminate around the animation. In a way, the piece is an operational manifestation of concept... sometimes it seems fantastic, other times it is a functional system — but in the end, it just works.

Paul Johnson was born in 1969 in Pasadena, CA. He has shown his work at Postmasters Gallery, New York (2002), the Seoul Museum of Art, Seoul (2002), ZKM, Germany (2002), The New Museum, New York, (2002), Eyebeam, New York (2002), Rare Gallery, New York (2000, 1999), the Galerie Yvon Lambert, Paris (2000, 1999), CRDC, Nantes (1998), P.S.1 Contemporary Art Center, New York (2001, 1997) and he has performed for the Whitney Biennial as a Sound Lab contributor, New York (1997).

WILLIAM KENTRIDGE

The process of seeing in — of seeing the face in the cloud — is the basis of the shadow work I have done over the last years. I take a sheet of black paper, tear it into three or four shapes and place them next to each other. Now, I could be a purist, defy nature, and say these are four abstract shapes made of black paper on a white ground, perhaps overlapping. But once I eliminate monasticism and dogmatics, things start to emerge. In one combination they are a dog, in another combination a man with a stick; I tilt a piece forward and he ages, I lean it back slightly and he gains in arrogance. Here the eye leads — it says, "Let me show you what I know of the world" and "This awkwardness in the shape in front of you is someone leaning on an uncomfortable hip." When Rembrandt or Picasso draws his woman teaching a child to walk, he is not saying, "I know what this looks like and will carry it out," but "Let me work with a looseness or openness that will allow to emerge what I cannot describe or give instructions for, but will recognize as it emerges" If I had said to myself "Let me make a shadow-figure of someone with a limp," I would have been hard-pressed to do it. The best I can do is to set in place strategies to allow this image of a limp to emerge.

This oscillation between openness and recognition is not limited to artists — it is fundamental to what it is to be sighted in the world. I did a workshop with 8-year-old scholars at my children's school in which they roughly cut or tore the elements of a vertebrate (a head, limbs, torso, pelvis) out of paper. Out of these shapes came a dog doing a somersault, a dinosaur rearing on its hind legs, a monster hiding its head behind its arm. If we had started the other way, none of them could have said or drawn what a dog doing a somersault looked like. But all could recognize it as it appeared before them, made by them.

In Plato's parable of the cave, the shadows — the only images the prisoners have ever seen, and which they understand to be reality — represent a deep ignorance and primitivism. Once a man is released from his chains, shown that these images are indeed only shadows cast by objects, and even dragged out of the cave to the world above, his obligation is to return to the prisoners to bring new knowledge and eventually lead them into the light. My interest in Plato's parable is twofold: for his prescient description of our world of cinema — his description of a world of people bound to reality as mediated through a screen feels very contemporary — but more particularly, in defense of shadows, and what they can teach us about enlightenment.

The very opening terms of Plato's metaphor are impossibly stated. If in fact one had been chained since childhood, unable to move one's head, as described of the viewers of the shadows, a total autism would result. The act of seeing, however — as opposed to receiving a pattern of light and shade on one's retina — is always a mediation between the received image and other knowledge. Shadows as objects, silhouettes or puppets make this mediation conscious and tell us things about seeing that are invisible in the light of the sun.

William Kentridge was born in 1955 in Johannesburg, South Africa, where he lives and works. Since participating in Documenta X in Kassel in 1997, solo shows of Kentridge's work have been hosted by the Museum of Modern Art, New York and MCA San Diego, and during 1998 and 1999 a survey exhibition of his work was seen in Brussels, Munich, Barcelona, London, Marseille and Graz. In 1999 he was awarded the Carnegie Medal at the Carnegie International 1999/2000. February 2001 saw the launch of a substantial survey show of Kentridge's work at the Hirshhorn Museum in Washington, traveling thereafter to New York, Chicago, Houston and Los Angeles during 2001/2002. He participated in Documenta 11 in 2002, with Confessions of Zeno, a shadow oratorio in collaboration with Handspring Puppet Company, composer Kevin Volans, and writer Jane Taylor.

ALEX KU
I made Tray thinking about how to break down a story into distinct emotional moments. In the past I preferred making stories which were more open-ended and spoke to an essentially unknowable quality about life and its interactions. To work in this more conventional way, breaking a story into narrative and emotional beats, made it possible to understand the characters' relationships, but tended for me to create a structure

which in the end limited both what could happen to the characters, — i.e., a happy ending, a sad one. Actions and consequences may drive a story, but do conflicts and resolutions really address other, more unanswerable aspects of our lived experience?
Now, thinking about it, an ironical turn would have been the most appropriate one. Because, ironically, something happened in my life which made Tray untrue. But, I guess, not always. Sometimes, you need stuff real bad to make you feel good. So you do something. And it's just a cartoon.

Alex Ku was born in Philadelphia in 1966 and lives in New York. His work has been recently seen in group shows at American Fine Arts, New York; Artists Space, New York; and P.S.1 Contemporary Art Center, New York, among others.

LIANE LANG
Animation gives life to the inanimate. It is a way of making performance art without performers. The performer may isolate gestures to examine their meaning, through exaggeration or excessive repetition. A similar process done with models removes all human identity and personality, race and gender. Animation can, by the mere fact of being entirely fake, make specific observations about behavior. Animation allows something that is clearly artificial to be identified as human or living by some physical resemblance or movement. The viewer projects desire and emotion onto the inanimate object, a response that is personal and sometimes intimate. Animation as a medium in art contains some unexplored territory. It allows for an amount of license to show things that are potentially disturbing or indecent and would be unpalatable or pornographic if they were real. Licking shows a plasticine head with a moist plasticine tongue licking a surface that may or may not be another body. The process of Licking starts off as a tentative, potentially erotic activity that gradually becomes more violent and unpleasant through its repetition. The activity of Licking is looked at in isolation, removed from all sense of sexual pleasure or interaction. A shift takes place from fascination and pleasure to disgust and discomfort. The inanimate nature of the protagonists renders empathy or identifi-

cation pointless. There are moments where the
figure and its movements allow the real and the
fake to become interchangeable yet indiscernible.

Liane Lang was born in 1973 in Munich, and lives
and works in London. Her work was featured in the
Liverpool Biennial (2002), and included in group
exhibitions at the Saatchi Gallery, London (2001)
and the Todd Gallery, London (1998). Solo shows
include Offspace, Vienna (2001) and Southfirst,
New York (2001).

KRISTIN LUCAS
My father used to play Keystone Cop super-8 films
backward on family movie night. When I went to
art school, I convinced him to loan me his early-
model Bell & Howell camera. I got really into the
mechanics of filmmaking and was instantly con-
sumed with the production of my own hand-drawn,
collogued, and special effectized, stop-action
animated shorts — kitchen table dioramas that
took up to 17-hours to shoot. Monty Python's
Flying Circus *animations by Terry Gilliam and*
film animations like A Trip to the Moon/ Le
Voyage dans la Lune *(1902) by George Melies blew*
my mind. I marveled over the simplicity and magic
of light blinking on a screen, perhaps best rep-
resented in movies like Wargames *(1983). I was*
similarly attracted to structuralist films and
interactive computer animation.
The hopes and fears of the future of a nation
were being provoked by a symphony of blinking and
strobing lights and frame rates. A tawdry effect
that dazzles and invokes fear among the masses. I
made Info-receptor *at a time when aspects of my*
life began to shift from analog to digital. There
was a lot of hype around metaphors like "informa-
tion superhighway" — which most of us still had
yet to experience in 1994, including myself. The
term "digital revolution" had not been coined
although there were a lot of concerns around
notion of authorship and loss of identity begin-
ning to surface. Info-receptor *is a flashy, low-*
budget, dim-witted, infomercial with a built-in
sense of irony. I shot half on videotape and half
on film, animating not only the subject but also
dramatizing the slogging shift from analog to
digital, sugar-coated with enthusiasm and ambiva-
lence.

Kristin Lucas was born in 1968 in Davenport,
Iowa, and lives and works in New York. She has
participated in residency programs within the
United States and abroad such as ARCUS, IBARAKI,
Japan (2000); World Views, New York (2000); and
P.S.1 National Studio Program, New York (1999).
Solo exhibitions of Lucas's work include:
Postmasters Gallery, New York (2001), ICA
Philadelphia, PA (2000), O.K Center for
Contemporary Arts Upper Austria, Linz (2000),
Kunsthaus Glarus (1999), and Windows Gallery,
Brussels (1998).

CHRISTINA MACKIE
Animation is a by-product of other activities —
certain things have to move, or involve slight
shifts over time. I like working on time slowed
down into frames, looking at the mechanics of
movement in visual terms, seeing where hiding or
missing something out makes the piece move bet-
ter. Time stretched to the slowest, smallest or
biggest unit. And images read in time allow
rhythm as an element of the visual.
Animated Drawing *was a last-minute sketch, a cal-*
ligraphic coda for a set of objects whose core
idea was that applying heat and pressure to rocks
and ice mimics the effect of time.

Christina Mackie was born in 1956, in Oxford,
England. She has presented solo exhibitions at
Henry Moore Institute, Leeds (2002), Magnani,
London (2000), CCA Kitakyushu (2000), AC Project
Room, New York (2001, 1999), The Showroom, London
(1999) and City Racing, London (1998). She also
participated in group shows at the Museum Ludwig,
Cologne (2000), the Sir John Soane Museum, London
(1999), the Musée d'Art Moderne de la Ville de
Paris (1996–97) and the Anthony D'Offay Gallery,
London (1996).

MELISSA MARKS
The Adventures of Volitia *began as a project in*
1993 with a series of drawings. I imagined that a
remnant of abstraction, a detachable Pollock drip
or mark, rose up, caught a glimpse of itself in
a mirror, and became self-aware. Next, this self-
conscious blob began to move. Volitia *was sudden-*
ly at once a sensational character and the
expression of herself in motion. Her adventures,
an ongoing, abstract narrative, describe the
idiosyncratic, emotional life of line.

Since 1993, the project has taken the form of drawings, paintings, and large scale wall-drawing installations. The Sorcerer's Swimming Pool (named for The Sorcerer's Apprentice, *Mickey Mouse's* famous segment in Fantasia) is the first Volitia installation to include animation. My work has always been influenced by cartoons and animation: the vivid artifice of cartoon color; the mock-heroic persona; that "pie in the face" mixture of violence and humor; and the simple idea that pictures move, so we watch. Experimenting with animation seemed a logical step. The surprise was in the discovery that the actual animations became "moving drawings," speaking more about drawing and line, while the color drawings, the more traditional works on paper, take on, as a subject, the history and style of animation.

Volitia (as in volition) is an aesthetically promiscuous abstract character. She is a hybrid hero: part Superman, part hot-house flower, part Eve — creation come to life. She is malleable, a constantly mutating fusion of what is inside and outside of herself. Born out of the animate line, a wanton self under pressure, Volitia exploded into action.

In her latest adventure, The Sorcerer's Swimming Pool, *Volitia* dives in with a new mentor and partner in emulsified imagery: water. Water is Volitia's close ally on the supercouncil of sentient abstractions. Like Volitia, water is restless, and in a state of perpetual change; defying gravity in evaporation, rushing back in new form as rain, seeping, crashing and advancing with an apparent will of its own. Even calm, water becomes reflection, inspiring reconsideration. With stasis as their enemy, Volitia and her ally taunt equilibrium. Provoked by the rectangle and seduced by the light, they take to the screen.

Melissa Marks was born in 1965 in New York City, where she currently lives and works. She has had solo exhibitions at the Nicole Klagsbrun Gallery, New York (1999) and The Aldrich Museum of Contemporary Art, Ridgefield, CT (1998). Marks has participated in group shows at Carnegie Mellon University, Pittsburgh, PA (2003), Gale Gates et al. Brooklyn, New York (2001), Schick Art Gallery, Skidmore College, New York (2001), and P.S.1 Contemporary Art Center, New York (2001, 1999).

JENNIFER AND KEVIN MCCOY
Our current work involves creating classification systems for popular narrative material. This material can be found in film, television, and literature. In some ways, animation is a very condensed form of narrative language in that each movement, set piece, or camera angle is drawn by the artist — nothing is accidental or incidental. This form also allows the maximum flexibility for creating the story's structure. The animation artist can make a huge narrative leap or impossible effect within just a few frames. For these reasons, our analysis of the cartoon format was very different than working with our other projects that examined live action material. For Every Anvil, we have created a database of extreme or violent gestures from Warner Brothers Looney Tunes cartoon classics. The process for the piece involves the meticulous dissection and analysis of over two thousand shot sequences. These sequences are then repackaged into categories like "every big hammer" or "every speed cloud" that the viewer may select and play. In some ways, the result is scrambled, in other ways it is highly ordered according to the logic of the database. Like fairy-tales, these cartoons employ formulas or archetypes of human behavior that make up the vast majority of narrative storytelling: hero vs. villain, intellect vs. strength, etc. These cartoons and fairytales constitute many of our earliest experiences with narrative. In Every Anvil we are interested in focusing on these formulas and on the brilliant animation techniques that bring them to life. A computer database can be presented in many forms. Often, it is hidden behind an interface from which the user makes choices and conducts searches. For Every Anvil, we decided to visualize the data-base. This visualization involves presenting "kits" which combine the playback mechanism (screen, player, speakers) with the media database. At a glance, one can see the whole range of categories available. In our work, these "media objects" represent a hybrid space between television and computers. They offer some of the interactivity of the computer and use the logic of the database to examine previous forms of cultural work.

Jennifer and Kevin McCoy (born 1967, Sacramento, CA and 1968, Seattle WA, respectively), have shown their work in New York at The Metropolitan

Museum of Art, P.S.1 Contemporary Art Center, Postmasters Gallery, The New Museum, and Smack Mellon (2000/ 2001), as well as projects at ZKM, Karlsruhe (2002), The Cornerhouse Gallery, Manchester (2001); Van Laere Gallery, Antwerp; and an upcoming show at F.A.C.T., Liverpool. In 2002, they received a Creative Capital Grant for Emerging Fields and in 2001 they received an award for New Media from the Colbert Foundation.

JONATHAN MONK

If you stare at a blank page for long enough it starts to move or if you
stare at a printed page for long enough it starts to move (even more)......
caricature or cartoon or comic book or
flip book or artist book or
animation cell or serial repetition or endless loop or twenty four frames a
second or more or less or one hundred cubes Cantz or Sol LeWitt or
Muybridge or Edward Ruscha or still images or sixteen millimeters or more or less or
post cards zooming in or
zooming out slow slow quick quick slow front to back back to front on its
side forever repeating (almost) or the same image equals slight movement or
color change or even "Six Years: The Dematerialization of the Art Object" in
only twenty seconds or forever over and over or under and above until it
vanishes from the screen through wear and tear and lines and forms equals
only twelve drawings filmed from the front to the back and back again
equalling one second of time flashing onto the wall breaking up the bright
light of nothing (repeat only slower and in a deeper voice).
P.S. simple mathematics.

Jonathan Monk was born in 1969 in Leicester, England. He has presented solo exhibitions at the Galleri Nicolai Wallner, (2002, 2001, 1998, 1995, 1994), at Casey Kaplan, New York (2001, 1999, 1997) and the Lisson Gallery, London (2003, 1998), Galerie Yvon Lambert, Paris (1998, 2000). He has participated in group shows at Kunsthalle Wien (2002), Kunsthalle Bern (2002), Kunsthalle

Nürnburg (2001), the Musée d'Art Contemporain, Avignon (2000), the 10th Swiss Sculpture Exhibition, Bienne (2000) and Le Magasin, Grenoble (1997).

JUAN MUÑOZ

Tom & Jerry embody what I most admire in art: an exact technique added to an arcane symbolism in such a balance that is rendered invisible for the spectator. The story is always the same, the story-teller is the one who really changes.
A mouse (or a cat) crashes against a door or is squashed by a falling wardrobe. Suddenly, its body is flattened and adopts the shape of a piece of paper. A window is opened and the breeze rocks it like a leaf falling from a tree. It reaches the floor and we confront an epiphany, a compression of life's meaning.
A hole, just like Jerry's, through which to disappear from this race, these narrow escapes from an endless amount of things falling, this running away from all kinds of objects. Maybe they are not exactly objects, but emotions, but they certainly seem to be collapsing all around! Yes, to have a hole to disappear.
Waiting for Jerry was built in 1991 as a gift for my daughter Lucía, who felt an unconditional solidarity with Jerry's need to defend himself from Tom's menacing presence. Nowadays, her younger brother Diego insists that this small and nervous mouse is a nightmare for the quiet and peaceful cat, who like Diego and myself, only wants to lay down and do nothing but watch cartoons.
Waiting for Jerry was constructed in the Van Abbemuseum, Eindhoven, in 1991, as a humorous comment on what I thought at the time was an increasing number of dark rooms in exhibitions. Seen with the added distance of time, I feel the piece has lost its social criticism but gained something else entirely.

Juan Muñoz was born in Madrid in 1953 and died in 2001. Solo exhibitions have been mounted at Tate Modern, London (touring) (2001); Louisiana Museum for Moderne Kunst, Humlbaek, Denmark, (2000); Marian Goodman Gallery, New York (2000, 1993); The Hirshhorn Museum, Washington, DC (1997); and Dia Center for the Arts, New York (1996), among many others. He participated in the

Carnegie International, Pittsburgh, PA, (1991); Documenta 9, Kassel (1992); and the Venice Biennale (1986, 1993, 1997).

DAMIÁN ORTEGA

Biologists consider Planet Solaris *a primitive formation, an ocean resulting from a dialectic development, a kind of gigantic cell, fluid and unique, that they call a "Pre-Biologic formation," a nervous system.*
Even a chronicler stated that the ocean was a distant relative of the electric eel! But in reality, not everyone was convinced that the Planet-Ocean was a living creature and even less a rational creature.
A monster gifted with reasoning, an Ocean-Brain offered itself to innumerable transformations, engendered by delirium.
That how it was born, the idea of the "Autistic-Ocean."
— Artist's English version of Solaris *(1961) by Stanislav Lem*

Damián Ortega was born 1967 in Mexico City. Solo exhibitions have been seen at the Institute of Contemporary Art, Philadelphia, PA and D'Amelio Terras Gallery, New York (both 2002). He has participated in group exhibitions at the Kiasma Museum of Contemporary Art, Helsinki; and the Witte de With Museum of Contemporary Art, Rotterdam (both 2001). He has also participated in the Tirana and Gwanju Biennials (2001, 2002.)

SVEN PÅHLSSON

Crash Course *examines our fear of the unpredictable and the unforeseen. This includes the negative occurrences, such as accidents and blind violence.* Crash Course *will reconstruct actual incidents and accidents from how they have been documented and filmed by the police from the police cruisers (squad cars). This video material was intended as visual proof to be used as evidence, but, in the tradition of the American entertainment industry, this footage has also been given to TV companies, provided to the TV viewer as entertainment with the added aspect of it being "real." 3D-modeled scenes are reconstructed and drawn from this documentary footage. Among the powerful possibilities of the 3D computer technology is the ability to accurately copy the parameters of reality and emulate actual physical properties (gravity, forces, collisions, etc.) By reconstructing these incidents in a very neutral and unbiased way,* Crash Course *will examine how the visual imagery governs how we perceive what really happened. This documentary imagery crosses the border between reality and fiction. Though the material is documentary, it is also well known from numerous Hollywood movies.*
Crash Course *will also look at the aspect of what occurs when one can't control what happens anymore, and one becomes victim of the surrounding actions. Another aspect of this project is the architectural road constructions and the different levels of space that these roads and junctions create. The roads and junctions also forms an intricate visual network, emulating in the physical reality the image of the electronic networks. There seem to be three different spaces; one is the space on top of the road, here you are usually in a traveling position moving at a speed. The other space is the space that connects to and surrounds the road systems. In this space you might live or work. The third space is the non-space, which exists under the roads and junctions, a leftover space where you aren't intended to be, and if you live here, you are outside society and space anyway.*
Music and soundtrack for Crash Course *is produced and composed by Erik Wøllo.*

Sven Påhlsson was born in 1965, in Lund, Sweden. Solo exhibitions have been mounted at Spencer Brownstone Gallery, New York (2001, 2002), Galeria Massimo De Carlo, Milan (2002), De Appel, Amsterdam (2002), Kunstnerforbundet, Oslo (2001), the Oslo Art Association (1999) and the Kunstnernes Hus Oslo (1997). Påhlsson participated in the Venice Bienniale, Nordic Pavillion (1997) and has been included in group shows at the Tate Modern, London (1998), the New Museum, New York (2002), Henry Art Gallery, Seattle (2002), Centre Pour L'image Contemporaine, Geneva (2002), Tentaciones, Madrid (2002), Museum of Art, Nuoro (2002), Moderna Museet, Stockholm (2002), Voges und Deisen, Frankfurt (2001), Momentum Biennale, Moss (1998) and the Staatsgalerie Kiel (1997).

PHILIPPE PARRENO
My name is Annlee! Annlee!
You can spell it however you want!
It doesn't matter! No it does not.

I was bought for 46000 Yen

46000 Yen, paid to a design character company.
"K" works!
I ended up, I ended up, like some others, in a
catalogue.
Proposed to cartoon producers and comic book edi-
tors.
Yea ! Like hum... like Drop dead in a comic
book!

Some other characters had the...
Some other characters had the possibility of
becoming a hero.
They had a long psychological description, a per-
sonal history,
material to produce a narration.
They were really expensive when I was cheap!
Designed to join any kind of story,
but with no chance to survive to any of them.

I / was never designed to survive...

It's true, everything I am saying is true!
Some names have been changed, to preserve the
guilty!

I / am / a product
a product freed from the market place I was sup-
posed to fill.
Drop dead in a comic book.
I will never forget.
I had just a name and an ID.

My name is Annlee!
My name is Annlee!
Spell it however you want!
It doesn't matter. No it does not.

After being sold, I was redesigned!
Funny! I can even say now! look!
That's how I used to be!
and this is how I look now.
It's like when you point out an old photo

Oh! Yeah! I forgot to tell you, the voice through
which
I'm talking to you now, was never my voice.
I have no voice! Her name is Daniela.
She is looking at me now!
She is a model. She is not used to speaking.

She is an image, just like me.
She is used to selling products when I've got
nothing to sell.
And I will never sell anything,
how can I? 'Cause I'm the product!

I was bought, but strangely enough I do not
belong to anybody.
I belong to whom is ever able to fill me with
any kind of imaginary material.
Anywhere out of the world.

I am an imaginary character.

I am no ghost, just a shell.

Philippe Parreno was born in 1964 in Oran, Algeria. He lives and works in Paris. Solo exhibitions have been organized at ARC, Musée d'Art Moderne de la Ville de Paris and Portikus, Frankfurt (2002). His work has been included in group exhibitions the Kunsthalle Zürich; Institute for Visual Culture, Cambridge, UK; SFMoMA, San Francisco, CA (all 2002/ 2003); the Stedelijk van Abbemuseum, Eindhoven (2003); and the Walker Art Center, Minneapolis, MN (2000). He participated in the 7th International Istanbul Biennal (2001) and appeared in D'Apertutto at the Venice Biennale in collaboration with Pierre Huyghe and Dominique Gonzalez-Foerster (1999).

JENNY PERLIN
Animation seems to me to most clearly articulate the particular properties of film: the 24 photographs per second; the persistence of vision which allows us to suspend our disbelief and to accept that a series of inanimate photographs is actually moving on the flat white screen before us. I occasionally hand-process a film. Other films I send to the lab for processing. The effect of hand processing in some ways counteracts the illusion of the animated image, and in other ways it emphasizes the mystery even more. Hand-processing allows me to get down and dirty with the celluloid, shoving ribbons of the stuff into a bucket of chemicals, treating the film as what it is — a bunch of plastic. The miracle then comes when the chemistry reveals what the light recorded on the film's surface. At the same time, my home laboratory adds a thick layer of nostalgia to the image. These films, developed as negatives, appear as though unearthed from old

basement boxes. They carry with them an air of the past and of loss. Hand processing also adds scratches. These scratches jump around on the surface of the filmed image, spontaneous animations in their own right. The final result of the hand processing in Lost Treasures came from my own carelessness — the beautiful colors that appeared because of my hasty processing — the chemicals continued to do their work long after I called it a day.

These are some of the reasons why I work with animation. To have a closer rapport with the wonderful clumsiness of film, with the imperfections of the homemade, and with the intimacy of capturing images in photographs, frame after frame after frame. Lost Treasures is a memorial to three women, each of whom taught me in different ways, and each of whom recently passed away. The film uses hand-processed high-contrast film, whose surface has been damaged by stains of unwashed chemistry, in an effort to express the disorientation of loss. The film's title and images come from the book Lost Treasures of Europe, a 1945 book of photographs of cultural monuments taken before they were destroyed in the Second World War.

Jenny Perlin was born in 1970 in Williamstown, Massachusetts and lives and works in New York. Perlin's films have screened nationally and internationally, including the Whitney Museum of American Art, New York; Havana Biennial, UCLA Hammer Museum, Los Angeles, CA; SF Cinematheque, Pacific Film Archive, San Francisco, CA; the Walker Art Center, Minneapolis, MN; and Kino Arsenal, Berlin. Her work has been included in group exhibitions at the Drawing Center, New York; P.S.1 Contemporary Art Center, New York; Apex Art, New York; the Queens Museum, New York; Shedhalle, Zurich; the Kunsthalle Exnergasse, Vienna; and the 2002 Swiss Expo. Awards include grants from the Civitella Ranieri Foundation, Wexner Center for the Arts, the Watson Foundation, and Artslink fellowships for collaborative projects in Eastern Europe.

LILIANA PORTER
The short video titled Drum Solo/Solo de Tambor is, in a sense, a sort of anti-animation. The movie begins with a long shot of a motionless plaster figurine of a "dressed" pig playing the drums. As we look at the image, we hear the sound of drums. Even if all along we are seeing that the pig is solid plaster, it is almost impossible not to conclude that the pig is the one making the sound.
These minimal theatrical situations that I create are placed against an empty, almost monochromatic background. This "intemporal" space allows for the possible communication between dissimilar characters and the simultaneity of disparate times. This video is a result of my experience with photography.
At the same time, video led me to a series of large Polaroids, many of them conceived as animation stills. There are subtle changes (movements) from one image to the next in diptychs or poliptychs. I am interested in the relationship between things and their representation, and I am attracted by the inevitable "mistakes" we make when we want to be precise in any description or definition. I am aware that all perception is an interpretation and there is a distance between the thing and the word that names it. The underlying concept is based on the intuition of a different (liberating) order of things.

Liliana Porter was born in 1941 in Buenos Aires, Argentina. Her most recent solo exhibitions include Galeria Espacio Minimo, Madrid (1998, 2000, 2001) Annina Nosei Gallery, New York (1999, 2000, 2002), Galeria Ruth Benzacar, Buenos Aires (2000) Galeria Brito-Cimino, Sao Paolo (2001) and Sicardi Gallery, Houston, TX (2002). She has participated in group shows at the Guggenheim Museum, New York (2001), Fundacion Telefonica, Madrid (2001); Fundació Juan Miró, Barcelona, (2001) Museo Nacional de Bellas Artes, Buenos Aires (2000), The Museum of Modern Art, New York (1992) and the New Museum of Contemporary Art, New York (1990).

POSSIBLE WORLDS
(JANINE CIRINCIONE AND MICHAEL FERRARO)
R/L, an interactive multi-media installation, is a meditation on the schism between what we

envision and what we see. R/L explores the dichotomy between utopian idealism vs. private realities, ideal public spaces vs. the dystopian function of real spaces. A kind of Waiting for Godot meets Calvino's Invisible Cities.

The installation presents a pair of animated characters who live in a tiny, abject world. We are voyeurs into the lives of these characters who behave as people do when they are alone and unwatched. They sit, they chitchat, they drink, they smoke, they pick their noses. Their conversations are filled with the mundane banalities and arguments that occur between couples who have too little to say — all of which reveals the small details that make up the fabric of everyday life. Viewers are encouraged to stay and hang with these characters for a while. Viewers' movements trigger sensors placed throughout the room. The viewers' behavior, then, is fed into a computer and processed so the characters respond to the stimuli in their environment. Thus the animated spectacle is composed on the fly, different for each viewer.

In real life we all live in small worlds, real worlds, with boredom, warts, problems and chaos yet we dream of the other ones, better ones — worlds that are so much better that they wouldn't allow people like ourselves to inhabit them.

In R/L the interactive relationship between the viewers and the animated characters is crucial. So is the interactive musical score that surrounds the piece which is based on John Cage's Time Bracket Notation. Cage's number pieces are a manifestation of "interactive" music — control of the musical experience is shared between composer and performer and changes with each performance. The "open-window-ness" of John Cage's number-pieces captures the coincidental nature of the individual and their environment… itself a kind of live self-performing experience.

Possible Worlds have shown their works in exhibitions at The Project, Los Angeles, CA (2002); P.S.1 Contemporary Art Center, New York (2001); The Wexner Center for the Arts, Columbus, OH (1998, 1994); Hosfelt Gallery, San Francisco, CA (2000); The Project, New York (1999, 1998); the Center of Contemporary Art, Macao, Hong Kong (1997); Postmasters Gallery, New York (1996); Il Triennale di Milano, Milan (1995); and The New Museum of Contemporary Art, New York (1993). They were recipients of the Artist-in-Residency Award at The Wexner Center for the Arts in 1993–94.

STORM VAN HELSING AND JIMMY RASKIN
The interview: (an excerpt)
Storm van Helsing: *Animation in its modern form was born in the laboratory of Dr. Frankenstein, but it has grown up in the virtual environments of contemporary monetary circulation. What began in the 19th Century as a mystico-scientific attempt to ascend to the power of the Gods, to be able to give the gift of life, has ended in the tawdry circumstances in which the suspicion is not only that we buy significance in our lives, but that we ourselves have been bought. If once animation was profoundly connected with certain kinds of freedom and desire, acting beyond the constraints of the actual world, a utopian realm whose lack of real material existence enabled actions, events and consequences unhindered by the dead weight of the actual world, today animation is considered a fallen medium relegated to the entertainment of feeble minds with magic and spectacle. Yet the more animation is presented to us today as a childish affair, of Saturday mornings and television, the more we can be certain that a profound manipulation is at work in disguise. Just as French philosopher Louis Althusser described ideologies as those false stories that are given to us about the real conditions of our lives, and relations with others, so today, what animates our lives and relations is the global capitalist monetary system. We are, all of us, turned into Frankenstein's monster, and live out our lives surrounded by the undead: by commodities and the arbitrary values of global monetary exchange. And so today, we sit with Jimmy Raskin, and will endeavour to discover the ways in which our puppet master operates our strings. Jimmy Raskin is an artist, performer and author who has investigated the nature of metaphor, through the convergence of the stories of Pinocchio and Nietzsche's* Thus Spoke Zarathustra. *His forthcoming book,* The Prologue, the Poltergeist and the Hollow Tree *is an attempt to provide closure on this investigation, which he has been conducting now for five years. We are currently in the offices of Jimmy Raskin, Jimmy, thank you for joining us. If you would be*

so kind, please set the scene for us. The Tightrope Walker: it would seem to me that he provides a compelling example of the division of intellectual and manual labor, and a prescient story about what we now know as the alienating effects of the spectacle. Please, the Tightrope Walker ...

Jimmy Raskin: *Well, I'll set the scene, ... I ... it was a very interesting introduction, I think I might be coming at it from another angle ...*

Storm van Helsing is a noted color theorist and curator. Famous for saying "Just because you can ... doesn't mean you should," van Helsing has been responsible for the temporary and permanent closure of numerous art institutions, including the "RECONSTRUCTION" of American Fine Arts gallery, New York, in 2001. His own account of this anti-exhibition policy was published in December 2001 by *Texte zur Kunst*.

Jimmy Raskin is an artist and writer residing in New York. He is the author of an upcoming book examining the tightrope walker from the prologue of *Thus Spoke Zarathustra* by Friedrich Nietzsche. Raskin's book is entitled *The Prologue, The Poltergeist, and the Hollow Tree*.

TERESA SEEMANN

How does one perceive a second? Video defines a second as thirty frames. Experientially, a second is about perceptually lost time defined through the act of looking and moving, such as "the second I turned my back" or "I blinked for a second and 'it' happened." "Second" is the position that comes after "first": the set-up for a linear narrative. Second also constitutes a follow-up action, a second chance or an "after."
Ducks (one second glance) features thirty nearly identical yellow, 2" x 1 1/2", plasticine ducks lined-up horizontally on a wall along with a video animation. Each duck has a slightly different facial expression relating to what precedes and follows it. The experience of walking past the ducks animates them. The video animation is a one-second motion loop of the ducks followed by a stationary pause. Each frame of the motion loop is comprised of the recorded image and sound of each individual duck for a total of thirty frames. Here technology provides the motion. What

prevails is the image and sound of a seemingly long, anarchic, one second glance.
Teresa Seemann was born in 1965 in Milwaukee, WI and lives in New York. Her work has been included in group exhibitions at P.S.1 Contemporary Art Center, New York, among others. Two-person shows with her collaborative partner David Galbraith have been seen at The New Museum of Contemporary Art, New York and the Soap Factory, Minneapolis, MN (both 2001).

KAREN YASINSKY

I use stop motion animation to focus on the details of characters' interactions. Through awkward movements and introspective gestures, the characters speak to our anxieties, frustrations and desires. I have always been fascinated by film's ability to intensely involve the viewer with the characters' state of mind in a way that allows the viewer to reflect back upon his/her reaction to that which was viewed. This was difficult for me to do in painting. But I wanted to work by myself so stop-motion animation fulfilled my conceptual needs and working method. I build the characters and get an idea of their personality through creating the body, clothing and sculpting the little heads. My process is such that the non-linear or suggested narrative evolves in the filming. Since it takes so long for a character to cross the set, 24 still frames per second, I am able to create their motivations for the movement that follows while filming. The suggested narrative can come about in a stream of consciousness that would be impossible to sustain if I had to explain it to actors or other people with which I was working. I don't have to rationalize the reasons for the characters' movements. In Fear, a 2-channel DVD projection, a man and a woman are confined to their respective screens, first in a landscape with a plane flying overhead and then inside of an airplane. The fear that possesses the characters comes from a schism between the desired and culturally acceptable or personally doable. This fear is not instigated from an outside force or object, it comes from within. This is shown through fantasy, both erotic and mundane. The music, sounds and subtle, awkward movements of the characters build to create a drama devoid of action, a repeating scene of irresolution.

Karen Yasinsky was born in 1965 in Pittsburgh, Pennsylvania. She will have a solo exhibition at Sprüth Magers Projekte, Munich (2003) and has had solo shows at UCLA Hammer Museum, Los Angeles, CA (2002) and Casey Kaplan, New York (1999, 1997, 1995). Yasinsky participated in *Cinematexas*, Austin, TX (2002), *The Brewster Project*, Brewster, NY (2002) and group shows at Museo Rufino Tamayo, Mexico City (2002), Brandenburgischer Kunstverein, Potsdam (2001), Portland Institute of Contemporary Art, Portland, ME (2001), Air de Paris (2000), P.S.1 Contemporary Art Center, New York (2000) and Artists' Space, New York (2000). She received a Guggenheim Fellowship and the Phillip Morris Emerging Artist Fellowship at the American Academy in Berlin in 2002 and will be included in the Rotterdam Film Festival (2003).

ON THE WEB

NATALIE BOOKCHIN
The Intruder *borrows the most popular form of entertainment consumed on computers, the game, to tell an unpopular story of unresolved gender-based conflicts.* The Intruder *is an experimental adaptation of a short story by Jorge Luis Borges, told in a hybrid form that exists on the border of computer and video arcade games and litera-ture. Players move forward through a linear nar-rative only by shooting, fighting, catching, or colliding with another character. Instead of win-ning a point, a player is rewarded with a piece of the narrative. At times the logic of games is subverted and the player must lose or receive a penalty in order to continue the story. Playing transforms readers into participants, who are placed inside of and implicated in the story — Borges's short tale of a tragic love triangle. Throughout the game, players' subject positions shift, and they must play on different and oppos-ing sides in the same story, paralleling the less-than-firm roles often performed in such real-life conflicts. The story is told in 10 game scenarios that together present a loose parallel narrative of a history of computer games.* The Intruder *begins with a reconstructed version of one of the earliest computer games, Pong, and*

ends with a war game, that, like its real-life counterpart, serves to simultaneously reinforce and abstract violence — in this instance, the narrative's violent end.

Natalie Bookchin lectures widely about art on the internet and exhibits her work both on the inter-net and in institutions such as MassMOCA, North Adams, MA; the Museum of Contemporary Art, Barcelona; LAMoCA, Los Angeles, CA; the Generali Foundation, Vienna; and the Shedhalle, Zurich. She is in the process of completing the first version of a Metapet, (metapet.net) an online game commissioned by Creative Time, New York in association with HAMACA, Barcelona. In 1999–2000, Bookchin organized <net.net.net>, an eight month series of lectures and workshops on art, activism and the Internet at CalArts, LAMoCA, and Laboratorio Cinematek in Tijuana. From 1998 to 2000, she was a member of the artist collective ®TMark. She is a 2001–2002 Guggenheim Fellow, a recent recipient of a California Arts Council Artist Fellowship, a Creative Capital Grant, Jerome Foundation/Walker Art Center Grant and a Daniel Langlois Grant among others. She is based in Los Angeles and teaches at CalArts.

YOUNG-HAE CHANG HEAVY INDUSTRIES
DAKOTA *is based on a close reading of Ezra Pound's* Cantos *part I and part II.*
At first, we didn't realize we were creating an animation. But it seems that by a certain new-media-art definition of things, when you use Flash you're doing animation. Someone suggested recently that we're doing motion graphics — O.K., except we don't really use graphics, just the Monaco font. We came upon moving text because we wanted a website, but quickly discovered we didn't know — or care to know — how web designers created online graphics, colors, photos, illus-trations, and text. Frankly, we dislike graphic design, and we also dislike interactivity, which are the two staples of web design, if not the web itself. Being artists, we like to do things wrong, or at least our own damn way. We ended up with a moving text synchronized to jazz, which was (and still is) all we could do.

YOUNG HAE CHANG HEAVY INDUSTRIES was founded in Seoul by Young-hae Chang, C.E.O., and Marc Voge,

C.I.O. It combines text with jazz to create Web pieces that present, for instance, a Homeric hero searching for sublime meaning in the insignificance of a life lived anywhere but where it seemingly counts; Asian businessmen and bar hostesses drinking the night away; a man who dies and is reborn as a stick; a Korean cleaning lady who is really a French philosopher; an illegal immigrant in a holding cell under the Justice Palace, in Paris; a woman who sexually embraces corporate monopoly; an evening with Sam Beckett in a bordello; a night roundup followed by an execution; the Riviera; Saul.

MARK DAGGETT
Browser Gestures *is an ongoing series of applications that reinterpret what an internet browser is. Along with the operating system, the browser presents the user with a series of metaphors. These metaphors envelop the user's experience, framing and contextualizing the data they view. My browsers reinterpret how a browser normally displays and navigates information for the user. The Blur Browser takes the page that the user requested and blurs the contents of the page until it becomes an abstract color field.*

Artist and designer Mark Daggett has developed Flavored Thunder for the past eight years as a series of ongoing experiments relating to the new media the "life-style." His work has recently been shown at the Whitney Museum's online *art.port;* Ars Electronica Festival, Linz; the New York Digital Salon; the Macros-Center, Moscow; the Transmediale Festival, Berlin; and the Princeton Art Museum, Princeton, NJ. Daggett lives and works in Los Angeles, California.

JOSHUA DAVIS
I've been reading a ton of painting essays on Jackson Pollock — where he had this brilliant quote of calling himself a painter, even though the brush never hit the canvas. Similarly, I would consider myself an artist, though I have no control over what this new engine outputs. In one sense I program the paints, the brushes, the canvas, the strokes, rules and boundaries. However, it is the machine that outputs the compositions and I, as the artist, am in a constant state of surprise and discovery because the machine may structure forms that I had never thought to execute.

Joshua Davis is a New York artist and technologist producing both public and private work on and off the Web. His site www.praystation.com won of the 2001 Prix Ars Electronica Golden Nica in the category "Net Excellence." He is currently an instructor at the School of Visual Arts in New York City.

ANDY DECK
I became interested in process as it applied to my painting around 1990. At the same time I began learning about computer programming. The initial impulse to use computers involved a desire to present all the developmental phases that my images went through before completion. So my use of animation is related to time-lapse photography more than character animation. This documentary aspect became more interesting, I believe, when the animations became collaborative around 1996. All of a sudden, it was less important for me to make images myself. I began to see my role more as providing a framework for other people — whether artists or not — to be creative and to confront new technology in the context of art.

Andy Deck works with collaborative drawing spaces, game-like search engines, problematic interfaces, and informative art. Deck has made art software since 1990, initially using it to produce short films. Since 1994, he has worked with the Web using the sites artcontext.net and andyland.net. An avid critic of corporate culture and militarism, Deck's hybrid news-art projects have sought to preserve available alternative media. Sensing the drift of the internet toward a marketing and entertainment medium, he works with open source software developers, optimizing his work for use with the Linux operating system, and publishing source code for much of his software. He lives and works in New York.

XETH FEINBERG
The Bulbo cartoons were created starting in 1998 as a personal experiment in Flash design and a satiric comment on the inherent limitations of online animation. At a time when the brave new hype of hi-tech Internet content was all the rage, simple black and white cartoons with inanely looping scratchy sound-tracks were actually more in tune the web's real speed. Technology put

us right back at the level of early Fleischer Brothers and Felix the Cat cartoons from the 1920's. (Personally, that suited me just fine.) In 20th Century, our retro-styled, bulb-headed protagonist traverses an animated timeline, covering 100 years of history in approximately 90 seconds.

Xeth Feinberg is an independent animator, cartoonist, and founder of Mishmash Media, Inc. Feinberg is the creator of the award-winning Bulbo series and numerous other animations and webtoons. He has worked with feature length animations, comic strips, and interactive "edutainment" CD-ROMs. He is the director, designer and animator of Showtime Network's popular Queer Duck series. He lives and works in New York.

ALEX AND MUNRO GALLOWAY
Day In, Day Out is a digital animation which simulates weather patterns, cycles of day and night, and seasonal and climatic change. It is designed as a networked environment which integrates information from weather sites on the web with the user's own IP address (used to access e-mail or the internet). The animation is launched from software contained on a CD-ROM. This program directs the user's PC to open up their browser to retrieve the most recent weather report in their area. With this information, it generates a visual approximation of what the weather looks like in the user's area. What appears on the screen of your personal computer is an artificial representation of the weather outside. Like watching the movement of clouds, the animation evolves slowly, adjusting to changes in the weather and the hour of day. The duration of the work is open-ended — the user determines the length of time they spend watching it. The animation is on-going, without beginning or end and without ever repeating itself. As a multi-user artwork, it can be viewed by several different users at the same time and appears different depending on where and when they are logged on.

Alex Galloway is a founding member of the software development group RSG (Radical Software Group) and is currently working on a web-based software product called Carnivore — based on the FBI software of the same name — that uses packet-sniffing technologies to create vivid depictions of raw data. Carnivore was awarded the Golden Nica Award for Net Vision at the Prix Ars Electronica 2002 in Linz. His work has been shown at the New Museum of Contemporary Art, New York; Eyebeam, New York; Princeton Art Museum, Princeton, NJ; MassMOCA, North Adams, MA; Walker Art Center, Minneapolis, MN; among others. As a scholar, Alex has written on digital media in popular and academic venues alike. His first book, PROTOCOL, or, How Control Exists After Decentralization, will appear in 2003 from MIT Press. He lives and works in New York, where he is an Assistant Professor of Media Ecology at New York University.

Munro Galloway's work has been included in several group exhibitions in New York and in solo shows at Murray Guy, New York; Giancarla Zanutti Arte Contemporanea, Milan; Galerie Martin Kudlek, Cologne; and DeChiara/Stewart Gallery, New York. In 2000, a work was commissioned by Air France and the Downtown Arts Festival. He lives and works in New York.

JODI
```
<SCRIPT>
var index = 0;
var yy = 0;
var xx = 0;
var Colors = new Array(„#000000", "#ffffff");
t.scrrr (120,100);
function qw() {
t.scrrr ( 0,10);
}
function zxc( ) {
window.setTimeout( „zxc()", 1);
xx = Math.round( 0 + Math.random() * 330);
yy = Math.round( 90 + Math.random() * 1);
t.scrrr(xx,yy);
changeBG();
}
function changeBG() {
index = Math.round(Math.random() *
(Colors.length-1)
); document.bgColor = Colors[index];
}
</SCRIPT>
<TITLE> %20 ./| ./| ./| ./| ./| ./| ./|
./| ./| ./| ./| ./|
```

```
./////
</TITLE></HEAD><BODY BGCOLOR="#000000"
TEXT="#ffffff" LINK="#00f0000" ALINK="#000000"
VLINK="#000000"
onload ="z x c ()"><K B D ><font
size=1><i><B><xDIR><S><PRE>
'xMM8R?!?MX!M$X %20[|[[[| /|\
[[]):]]]][][][][]||[[]]]|||[]]{{|}[\{[}|[\][[||{]-|||||||||]
]][[[]
%20[|[[[| /|\
[[]):]]]][][][][]||[[]]]|||[]]{{|}[\{[}|[\][[||{]-||||||||||]
]][[[]
%20[|[[[| /|\
[[]):]]]][][][][]||[[]]]|||[]]{{|}[\{[}|[\][[||{]-|||||||||]
]][[[] %20[|[[[| /|\
[[]):]]]][][][][]||[[]]]|||[]]{{|}[\{[}|[\][[|||{]
```

JOHN KLIMA

Interactive, real-time 3D animation provides the artist with a conceptually limitless studio, an environment where anything imaginable can be realized either in a meta-form or as a physical object. With real-time animation, the artist can create a gigantic, site-specific installation right down to every nut and bolt, provide a compelling and realistic VR walkthrough, and send off blueprints to a fabricator for an estimate. At the same time, the artist can create an inscrutable object that exists, and only exists, on a Gameboy handheld computer. The elements of both can be combined, so the physical and meta components heighten and extend each other. Networks allow individuals at remote locations to have shared experiences in real time. Glasbead *makes use of network technologies to create a multi-user on-line musical object. Part instrument, part toy, part game,* Glasbead *blurs the distinctions, leveraging each to create a unified and compelling audio, visual, and interactive experience.* Glasbead *enables players to create a shared aesthetic environment where each player contributes to the result. The challenge in creating* Glasbead *was to make it simple enough for anyone to create a pleasing sound, yet complex enough to be "composed" for.*

John Klima's work has been exhibited at Postmasters Gallery, NY; The Whitney Museum of American Art and the 2002 Whitney Biennial, New York; Eyebeam, New York; the New Museum of Contemporary Art, New York; the Museum for Communication, Bern, Switzerland; the NTT InterCommunication Center, Tokyo, Japan; and many international festivals. He lives and works in New York.

GOLAN LEVIN AND CASEY REAS

Typing can be thought of as percussive spatial action — a play of tiny thoughts scattered onto a tightly organized grid. Typing is also a kind of speech, spoken through the fingers with flashing rhythms and continuous gestures. Dakadaka *is an interactive applet that explores these ideas by combining positional typographic systems with an abstract dynamic display. Through mapping the grid of the computer keyboard to the screen,* Dakadaka *reflects these fleeting performances back to us, reminding us of their gestural and continuous qualities.*

Golan Levin is an artist, composer, performer and engineer whose work spans a variety of online, installation and performance media. *Dialtones*, a concert where the sounds are wholly performed through the carefully choreographed dialing and ringing of the audience's own mobile phones, was presented in Ars Electronica in 2001. Levin was granted an Award of Distinction in the Prix Ars Electronica for his Audiovisual Environment Suite interactive software and its accompanying audio-visual performance, *Scribble* in 2000. Levin works and teaches in New York.
Casey Reas explores abstractions of biological and natural systems through software art, prints, and animation. Reas has lectured and exhibited in Europe, Asia, and the United States. His work has recently been shown at the American Museum of the Moving Image, New York; Ars Electronica, Linz; IAMAS, Ogaki; and The Museum of Modern Art, New York. In 2001, Casey received his M.S. degree in Media Arts and Sciences from the MIT Media Laboratory, where he was a member of John Maeda's Aesthetics and Computation Group (ACG). Reas is currently an associate professor at the newly founded Interaction Design Institute Ivrea in Italy. With Ben Fry of the ACG, he is developing *Proce55ing*, a context for learning programming and other fundamentals of the electronic arts.

SEBASTIAN LUETGERT

"Can we already grasp the rough outlines of the coming forms, capable of threatening the joys of

marketing? Many young people strangely boast of being 'motivated;' they re-request apprenticeships and permanent training. It's up to them to discover what they're being made to serve, just as their elders discovered, not without difficulty, the telos of the disciplines. The coils of a serpent are even more complex that the burrows of a molehill." (Gilles Deleuze, Postscript on the Societies of Control)

The Coils of the Serpent is a 30 minute sequence of 120 animated gif images, each of which repeatedly loops two different corporate logos for 15 seconds. The logos have been copied from the companies' websites, and the sequence has been realized with JavaScript and PHP. The work is free of copyright and may be reproduced, distributed and modified without any legal restrictions.

The Coils of the Serpent is neither exactly affirmative nor critical. Rather than a statement, it is an attempt to "grasp the rough outlines of the coming forms" of the societies of control — the integrated spectacle of "global" ethics and "corporate" aesthetics'

Sebastian Luetgert was born 1972 in Bielefeld, Germany. He lives in Berlin, working as a writer, programmer and artist.

PANAJOTIS MIHALATOS

This small shockwave is not a representation of some floor plan with rotating panels but an attempt to create a kind of "digital space." The idea behind it was that complexity can emerge out of a field of monotonous repetition (the grid, an anti-narrative organizing principle that had a great impact on architecture with ambiguous results) of a single element, as long as this element has some degree of freedom. That is also the foundation of the digital, where everything is created out of the elemental distinction of the binary system. Complexity and a formation of dynamic systems also require interaction, (a characteristic of games) and that is why I wanted to have this game quality. The idea of placing the panels in that particular pattern came from a very old game (mid-Eighties) for the Commodore 64 computer. I had already started to look back at the origins of computer games at an age where there was limited capacity for fancy graphics and all the weight of the game design was placed not on representation but on interaction, abstraction and what is called gameplay. The game was seen as

an open problematic field and not a narration where you happen to participate. Similar ideas have been expressed in architecture like in the case of the Sonsbeek pavilion by Aldo van Eyck, The Free University of Berlin By Josic, Candillis and Woods, and the Museum of São Paolo by Lina Bo Bardi.

MARK NAPIER

My work is not animation in the traditional sense of that term. It is animated, meaning that it moves over time, but it is not animation in the traditional sense of a linear sequence of predetermined images. p-Soup uses algorithms to generate graphical events on screen whenever a visitor to the piece clicks within the artwork. There are nine graphical "flavors" that the visitor can choose from, but there are endless possibilities to the way these can be combined on the screen. The work is animated the way ripples animate the surface of a pool. The ripples are simple circular waves, yet they overlap to create unpredictable and varied patterns. I enjoy the element of surprise that comes from this approach. At times, the artwork does things I never expected. In a multi-user piece like p-Soup, I am surprised to find that someone else is participating in the work at the same time that I am. For a moment I can communicate with another person through the work. These actions are not possible with a static medium like painting or linear pre-determined media like video or film. p-Soup is about the human creative impulse, the desire to touch and affect the world. The idea of touch plays a large part in the work. When humans communicate through electronic media like the web, we lose the sense of touch; there is nothing for us to get our hands on. Similarly, when we view art (another medium of communication), we are not allowed to touch the artwork; the object may be altered by the visitor's hand. p-Soup is about creating a touchable artwork in a world where there is no physical object to touch.

In p-Soup, a virtual surface is disturbed by the click of the visitor's mouse, as if they are touching a surface of water, creating pulsing ripples that spread and decay over time. Visitors create a design that grows and then fades away. They do not own this design, as it will fade in minutes, and may be altered by other visitors that are using the piece at the same time. p-Soup creates a place where artwork can exist for a fleeting moment, created between people as they touch a shared virtual surface. The work is blank when people arrive to it, and is activated, turned into 'art' by their touch. When the people leave, the artwork returns to a still quiet blue, and waits.

Mark Napier has been creating artwork exclusively for the web since 1995. Napier is known for his wide range of internet projects including *The Shredder*, an alternative browser that dematerializes the web, *Digital Landfill*, an endless archive of digital debris, and *Feed*, a web filter commissioned by the San Francisco Museum of Modern Art. A recipient of a NYFA Fellowship and a grant from the Greenwall Foundation, Napier has been commissioned to create net artwork for SFMOMA, the Whitney Museum of American Art, the Guggenheim Museum, and Altoids.com. His work has been shown in the Whitney Museum of American Art and the 2002 Whitney Biennial, New York; SFMOMA, San Francisco; Zentrum fur Kunst und Medientechnologie, Karlsruhe; the Walker Art Center, Minneapolis, MN; and new media festivals in Germany, Italy, Denmark and South America. He lives and works in New York.

MOUCHETTE

"Once, on Mouchette's site, you killed a fly... It was just a button that you clicked, but then you heard some crying and sobbing and a text was being typed: little-fly- Mouchette — crying over her own death — was calling you a killer and asking: 'How can I write this since I'm dead?' You wrote an answer and sent it. Now your answer appears in the Lullaby for a Dead Fly *with your name and the date you sent it, together with the answer of hundreds of other visitors. All these texts stream slowly by, downloaded from Mouchette's web server, and while you're reading them you fall into a deep meditation about death, the essence of writing, the internet and the short existence of flies."*
— K. Pettitt

Mouchette has exhibited her work at the Maison Européenne de la Photographie, Paris; the Stedelijk Museum, Amsterdam; the New Museum of Contemporary Art, New York; the Museo de Arte Carrillo Gil, Mexico City; the Biennale de Montreal; the Candy Factory, Tokyo; as well as many festivals in Brazil, Slovenia, Germany, the Netherlands, Croatia, and the United States. She lives and works in Amsterdam.

WORD.COM AND ERIC ZIMMERMAN

SiSSYFiGHT 2000 *is not an animated work in the traditional sense.* SiSSYFiGHT 2000 *is a game. Unlike pregenerated media like film and video, games exist as sets of rules — as procedures that are set into motion by the participation of the players as they play the game. In the case of* SiSSYFiGHT, *this act of play occurs on many levels: social interaction, strategic decision-making, narrative role-playing, and perverse critique of many of the conventions of computer gaming. As players interact with the structures of* SiSSYFiGHT 2000 *and play the game, they are in a sense algorithmically generating an improvisational animation. The drama that occurs in a game of* SiSSYFiGHT *is an emergent property of the experience, an effect of the process of play, rather than something pre-coded by the designers of the game. Thus the complex operation of desire and drug-like addiction in* SiSSYFiGHT 2000. *The top* SiSSYFiGHT *players have played the game thousands of times. How many times have you seen your favorite animation?*

Eric Zimmerman is a game designer, artist, and academic exploring the emerging field of game design. Zimmerman is CEO and co-founder of gameLab, a game development company based in New York, which has won Webby Award nominations and a nomination for a GDC Game Developers Choice award. Other projects include *SiSSY FiGHT 2000* (www.sissyfight.com) developed with Word.com, and *STRAIN*. In 1999, Zimmerman organized RE:PLAY, a series of events on game design and game culture that included an online and real-world conference and a book, and he co-authored a textbook on game design with Katie Salen published by MIT Press in 2002. Zimmerman has also exhibited his work at Artists Space, New York; Sara Meltzer Gallery, New York; the Center for Contemporary Arts, Grenoble; and the Bellevue Museum, Seattle, WA. Zimmerman is currently an Adjunct Professor at New York University's Interactive Telecommunications Program. He has been a Visiting Lecturer at MIT's Comparative Media Studies Program, and at Parsons School of the Arts' MFA Digital Design Program.

Captions

(12) Juan Muñoz, *Waiting for Jerry*, 1991, installation with audio CD

(26) Haluk Akakçe, *Illusion of the First Time*, 2002, triple channel DVD. Special thanks to The Whitney Museum of American Art at Phillip Morris, New York

(40) Francis Alÿs, *The Last Clown*, 2000, installation with video projection, drawings, paintings and mixed media

(46) Francis Alÿs, *Song for Lupita*, 1998, installation with video projection, record player and mixed media

(50) Pierre Huyghe, *No Ghost Just a Shell: Two Minutes out of Time*, 2000, video installation with single channel DVD

(52) Pierre Huyghe, *One Million Kingdoms*, 2001, video installation with single channel DVD

(56) Philippe Parreno, *No Ghost Just a Shell: Anywhere Out of The World*, 2000, video installation with single channel DVD

(60) Liam Gillick, *No Ghost Just a Shell: AnnLee You Proposes*, 2001, single channel DVD

(68) Sven Påhlsson, *Crash Course*, 2000, single channel DVD

(78) Jeremy Blake, *Guccinam*, 1999, single channel DVD

(88) Karen Yasinsky, *Fear*, 2001, double channel DVD

(94) Melissa Marks, *The Adventures of Volitia: The Sorcerer's Swimming Pool*, 2001: *Volitia Makes Waves* and *Double Waterfall*, two single channel DVDs

(100) William Kentridge, *Shadow Procession*, 1999, single channel DVD

(114) William Kentridge, *Untitled (video reversals)*, 2002, charcoal, pigment and turpentine on paper

(122) Angus Fairhurst, *Normal/Distorted/Superimposed*, 2001, single channel DVD

(124) Jonathan Monk, *Sol Le Witt Lines & Forms Yvon Lambert 1989 front to back back to front with blank space ten to one forever*, 2000, 16 mm film

(126) Jenny Perlin, *Lost Treasures*, 1999, 16 mm film

(130) Simon Henwood, *Johnny Pumpkin*, 2000, installation including single channel VHS and laser-print on vinyl

(132) Peggy Ahwesh, *She Puppet*, 2001, single channel DVD

(134) Liliana Porter, *Drum Solo/ Solo De Tambor*, 2000, single channel DVD

(138) Liane Lang, *Licking*, 2000, single channel VHS

(140) top to bottom:
Damián Ortega, *Planeta Salvaje*, 2001, video installation with double channel VHS

Oladélé Ajiboyé Bamgboyé, *Body*, 2000, video installation with single channel DVD

Christina Mackie, *Animated Drawing*, 1999, single channel DVD

(144) top to bottom:
Claudia Hart, *More Life*, 2001, single channel DVD

Teresa Seemann, *Ducks (one second glance)*, 2000, mixed media with single channel VHS

David Galbraith, *Figuring By Design*, 1999, single channel VHS

Jennifer and Kevin McCoy, *Every Anvil*, 2001, custom boxes which play archive of cartoon visuals and sounds

(148) top to bottom:
Kristin Lucas, *Info-receptor*, 1994, single channel VHS

Storm van Helsing and Jimmy Raskin, *Hollow Tree: The Interview*, 2001, installation including backdrop paper, paint, and single channel VHS

Alex Ku, *Tray*, 2001, single channel VHS

Possible Worlds (Janine Cirincone + Michael Ferraro), *RL*, 2001, mixed media installation

FOLLY
(all works single channel VHS)

(158) top to bottom:
J. Tobias Andersson, *879*, 2002; *One Moment*, 2001
Avish Khebrehzadch, *Red Hair*, 2000
Ingrid Bromberg. *Fever*, 1999
Sarah Ciraci, *Rapimenti # 1*, 2001
Maureen Connor, documentation of the installation *Growing Older*, 1999

(159) top to bottom:
Melanie Crean, *Alpha Omega*, 1998
Deborah Davidovits. *Shadow Plays, Vols. 1 and 2*, 2001
Rory Hanrahan, *Courtroom Drama*, 2000
Tim Hirzel, *My Life As Four*, 2001
Omar Lewis & Jason Cooper, *T.O.R.A.L. (The only real artists left)*, 2001

(160) top to bottom:
Daniel Lefcourt, *Site 11*, 2001
Cecilia Lundquist, *Rebus*, 2000
Rupert Norfolk, *Untitled (Even Hundred)*, 2001
Diego Perrone, *I Verdi Giorni*, 2000
Root R (Shingo Suzuki), *Loop*, 1999, *Reflect*, 2001
Joe McKay, *Lucky Five*, 2001

(161) top to bottom:
Jonathan Rosen, *Cartoon Cavalcade, Debauchery*, 2001
Kathy Rose, *She, Oriental Interplay*, 2000
Jason Schiedel, *A Rescue*, 1999
Matthew Suib, *Hounds on Fire*, 2001
Scott Teplin, *Lapse*, 2001
Xana Kudriacev-DeMilner, *Vista 1*, 2001

Works in the Exhibition

Peggy Ahwesh
She Puppet, 2001
Single channel DVD
Courtesy the artist

Haluk Akakçe
White on White, 2002
Single channel DVD
Courtesy the artist and Deitch Projects, New York

Black on Black, 2002
Single channel DVD
Courtesy the artist and Deitch Projects, New York

Francis Alÿs
Song for Lupita, 1998
Installation with video projection, record player and mixed
media
Courtesy the artist and Lisson Gallery, London

Oladélé Ajiboyé Bamgboyé
Body, 2000
Video installation with single channel DVD
Courtesy the artist and Thomas Erben Gallery, New York

Jeremy Blake
Guccinam, 1999
Single channel DVD
Courtesy the artist and Feigen Contemporary, New York

Angus Fairhurst
Normal/Distorted/Superimposed, 2001
Single channel DVD
Courtesy the artist and Sadie Coles HQ, London

David Galbraith
Figuring By Design, 1999
Single channel VHS
Courtesy the artist

Liam Gillick
No Ghost Just a Shell: AnnLee You Proposes, 2001
Single channel DVD
Courtesy the artist and Casey Kaplan, New York

Claudia Hart
More Life, 2001
Single channel DVD
Courtesy the artist

Simon Henwood
Johnny Pumpkin, 2000
Installation including single channel VHS
and laser-print on vinyl
Courtesy the artist

Pierre Huyghe
No Ghost Just a Shell: Two Minutes out of Time, 2000
Video installation with single channel DVD
Courtesy the artist and Marian Goodman Gallery, Paris / New York

Paul Johnson
Monocular Projector, 1995
Mixed media
Courtesy the artist and Postmasters Gallery, New York

Binocular Projector, 1995
Mixed media
Courtesy the artist and Postmasters Gallery, New York

Binocular Projector v.2, 1995
Mixed media
Collection Peter Surace

Flashlight Projector, 1998
Mixed media
Courtesy the artist and Postmasters Gallery, New York

Mounted Flashlight Projector, 1998
Mixed media
Collection James Healy

Horizontal Projector, 1998
Mixed media
Courtesy the artist and Postmasters Gallery, New York

Hoover Wet and Dry, 2001
Mixed media
Collection Carol Chow

Consoles, 2002
5 altered computer consoles
Courtesy the artist and Postmasters, New York

William Kentridge
Memo, 1994
Single channel DVD
Courtesy the artist and Marian Goodman Gallery New York /
Paris

Shadow Procession, 1999
Single channel DVD
Courtesy the artist and Marian Goodman Gallery New York /
Paris

Untitled (video reversals), 2002
Charcoal, pigment and turpentine on paper
Courtesy the artist and Marian Goodman Gallery New York /
Paris

Portage, 2001
Leporello book
Lithograph collage on found pages
Courtesy the artist

Alex Ku
Tray, 2001
Single channel VHS
Courtesy the artist

Liane Lang
Licking, 2000
Single channel VHS
Courtesy the artist

Kristin Lucas
Info-receptor, 1994
Single channel VHS
Courtesy the artist

Christina Mackie
Animated Drawing, 1999
Single channel DVD
Courtesy the artist and Magnani, London

Melissa Marks
The Adventures of Volitia: The Sorcerer's Swimming Pool, 2001
- *Volitia Makes Waves*, single channel DVD
- *Double Waterfall*, single channel DVD
- *Volitia Retreats*, color pencil on paper
- *Volitia Wades In*, color pencil on paper
Courtesy the artist and Nicole Klagsbrun Gallery, New York

Jennifer and Kevin McCoy
Every Anvil, 2001
Custom boxes which play archive of cartoon visuals and sounds
Courtesy the artists and Van Laere Contemporary Art, Antwerp.
Collection of Wim Delvoye, Ghent

Jonathan Monk
Sol Le Witt Lines & Forms Yvon Lambert 1989 front to back back to front with blank space ten to one forever, 2000
16 mm film
Courtesy the artist and Galerie Yvon Lambert, Paris

Juan Muñoz
Waiting for Jerry, 1991
Installation with audio CD
Courtesy Marian Goodman Gallery, New York / Paris

Damián Orteǧa
Planeta Salvaje, 2001
Video installation with double channel VHS
Courtesy the artist, kurimanzutto Gallery, Mexico City and D'Amelio Terras Gallery, New York

Sven Påhlsson
Crash Course, 2000
Single channel DVD
Courtesy the artist and Spencer Brownstone Gallery, New York

Philippe Parreno
No Ghost Just a Shell: Anywhere Out of The World, 2000
Video installation with single channel DVD
Courtesy Air de Paris, Paris, and Friedrich Petzel, New York

Jenny Perlin
Lost Treasures, 1999
16 mm film
Courtesy the artist

Liliana Porter
Drum Solo/ Solo De Tambor, 2000
Single channel DVD
Courtesy the artist and Annina Nosei Gallery, New York

Possible Worlds
(Janine Cirincone + Michael Ferraro)
RL, 2001
Mixed media installation
Courtesy the artists and The Project, New York / Los Angeles

Teresa Seemann
Ducks (one second glance), 2000
Mixed media with single channel VHS
Courtesy the artist

Storm van Helsing and Jimmy Raskin
Hollow Tree: The Interview, 2001
Installation including backdrop paper, paint, and single channel VHS
Courtesy the artists and American Fine Arts, New York

Karen Yasinsky
Fear, 2001
Double channel DVD
Courtesy the artist

ON THE WEB

Natalie Bookchin
The Intruder, 1999
www.calarts.edu/~bookchin/intruder/
Courtesy the artist

Mark Daggett
Blur Browser, 2001
www.flavoredthunder.com/dev/browser-gestures
Courtesy the artist

Joshua Davis
Machine # 09182001, 2001
Courtesy the artist

Andy Deck
Open Studio, 2001
In collaboration with Jenny Chapman
www.artcontext.org/draw
Courtesy Artcontext

Xeth Feinberg
Bulbo in the 20th Century, 2000
www.bulbo.com/bmovies/bulbo-20th.html
Courtesy the artist
Alex and Munro Galloway
Day In, Day Out, 2001

Networked software application
Courtesy the artists and Murray Guy Gallery, New York

JODI
ASDFG, 1999
asdfg.jodi.org
Courtesy the artists

John Klima
Glasbead, *2000*
www.glasbead.com
Courtesy the artist

Golan Levin and Casey Reas
Dakadaka, 2000
acg.media.mit.edu/projects/dakadaka/dakadaka.html
Courtesy the artists

Sebastian Luetgert
The Coils of the Serpent part 1, 1999–2001
rolux.org/index.php3
Courtesy the artist

Panajotis Mihalatos
Flexible Planning, 2000
users.otenet.gr/~pan_mi/drelb.htm
Courtesy the artist

Mouchette
Lullaby for a Dead Fly, 2000
www.mouchette.org/fly
Courtesy the artist

Marc Napier
P-Soup, 2000
www.potatoland.org/p-soup
Courtesy the artist

YOUNG-HAE CHANG HEAVY INDUSTRIES
DAKOTA, 2001
www.yhchang.com/dakota.html
Courtesy the artists

Word.com and Eric Zimmerman
SiSSYFiGHT 2000, 2000
www.sissyfight.com
Courtesy the artists

FOLLY

J. Tobias Anderson, *879*, 2002; *One Moment*, 2001
Courtesy the artist

Ingrid Bromberg, *Fever*, 1999
Courtesy the artist

Sarah Ciraci, *Rapimenti # 1*, 2001
Courtesy the artist and Galeria Emi Fontana, Milan

Maureen Connor, documentation of the installation *Growing Older*, 1999
Courtesy the artist

Melanie Crean, *Alpha Omega*, 1998
Courtesy the artist

Deborah Davidovits, *Shadow Plays, Vols. 1 and 2*, 2001
Courtesy the artist

Rory Hanrahan, *Courtroom Drama*, 2000
Courtesy the artist

Tim Hirzel, *My Life As Four*, 2001
Courtesy the artist

Avish Khebrehzadch, *Red Hair*, 2000
Courtesy the artist

Xana Kudriacev-DeMilner, *Vista 1*, 2001
Courtesy the artist

Daniel Lefcourt, *Site 11*, 2001
Courtesy the artist

Omar Lewis & Jason Cooper, *T.O.R.A.L. (The only real artists left)*, 2001
Courtesy the artists

Cecilia Lundquist, *Rebus*, 2000
Courtesy the artist

Joe McKay, *Lucky Five*, 2001
Courtesy the artist

Rupert Norfolk, *Untitled (Even Hundred)*, 2001
Courtesy the artist

Diego Perrone, *I Verdi Giorni*, 2000
Courtesy the artist and Casey Kaplan Gallery, New York

Root R (Shingo Suzuki), *Loop*, 1999, *Reflect*, 2001
Courtesy the artist

Kathy Rose, *She, Oriental Interplay*, 2000
Courtesy the artist

Jonathan Rosen, *Cartoon Cavalcade, Debauchery*, 2001
Courtesy the artist

Jason Schiedel, *A Rescue*, 1999
Courtesy the artist

Matthew Suib, *Hounds on Fire*, 2001
Courtesy the artist

Scott Teplin, *Lapse*, 2001
Courtesy the artist

Florian Zeyfang, *Transmission Attempts*, 1998
Courtesy the artist

P.S.1 Contemporary Art Center

Museum of Modern Art affiliate

22-25 Jackson Ave at 46th Ave

Long Island City, New York 11101

T: 718.784.2084

F: 718.482.9454

mail@ps1.org

www.ps1.org

The programs at P.S.1 Contemporary Art Center are made possible in part by the New York City Department of Cultural Affairs, the Office of the Borough President of Queens, and the Council of the City of New York.

KW — Institute for Contemporary Art
Kunst-Werke Berlin e.V.
Auguststr. 69
10117 Berlin
T: ++49.30.24.34.59.0
F: ++49.30.24.34.59.99
Info@kw-berlin.de
www.kw-berlin.de

Board of Directors
Eike Becker, President
Eberhard Mayntz, Vice President
Kate Merkle, Treasurer
Klaus Biesenbach, Founder and Artistic Director
Alanna Heiss, Curatorial Advisor
Katharina Sieverding, Artistic Advisor

Members of the Board
Marina Abramovic
Lawton Fitt
Jenny Goetz
Egidio Marzona

Staff
Artistic Director: Klaus Biesenbach
Associate Curators: Anselm Franke, Daniel Marzona
Exhibition Manager: Katrin Lewinsky
Curatorial Assitant: Sine Bepler
Managing Director: Beate Barner
Assistant to the Manager: Monika Grzymislawska
Press Officer: Maike Cruse
Publications: Vanessa Adler
Technical Director: Matten Vogel
Accountant: Imke Schwärzler
Office: Marlies Krause-Pitrowski
Building: Peter Ohm, Dieter Sielaff
Head of Security: Udo Klink
Interns: Alexandra Toland, Jan Philip Müller
Custodians: Esther Gaelle Nsiani Youansi, Renate Wenzel

The cultural programs of Kunst-Werke Berlin e.V., Institute
for Contemporary Art, are made possible thanks to the support
of the Senatsverwaltung für Wissenschaft, Forschung und
Kultur, Berlin and additional support by P.S.1 Contemporary
Art Center, a MoMA affiliate.
Special thanks to Stiftung Deutsche Klassenlotterie.

The exhibition at KW — Institute for Contemporary Art was made
possible with the support of Hauptstadtkulturfonds, Berlin.

Additional support for the catalogue is provided by
Dornbracht Armaturenfabrik, Iserlohn/Germany.

Acknowledgements: Nomad Worldwide LLC; The Mexican Cultural
Institute; The Italian Cultural Institute, New York; Florence
Bonnefous and Galerie Air de Paris; Spencer Brownstone
Gallery, New York; Sadie Coles HQ, London; D'Amelio Terras,
New York; Deitch Projects, New York; Thomas Erben Gallery,
New York; Richard Feigen and Feigen Contemporary, New York;
Marian Goodman Gallery, New York and Paris; Galerie Yvon
Lambert, Paris; Casey Kaplan Gallery, New York; Galerie
Kurimanzutto, Mexico City; Harvestworks; Lisson Gallery,
London; Annina Nosei Gallery, New York; Ocularis Cinema
Williamsburg Style; Friedrich Petzel Gallery, New York;
Postmasters Gallery, New York; Van Laere Contemporary Art,
Antwerp; Whitney Museum of American Art at Phillip Morris,
New York.

Thanks to: Rosa and Gilberto Sandretto, Wolfgang Abramowski,
Kieran Argo, Yona Backer, Mary Lea Bandy, Judith Barry,
Leonard Baskin, Judith Becker, Giannalberto Bendazzi, Lutz
Bertram, Marco de Blois (Cinemathéque Québecoise), John
Canemaker, Maike Cruse, Wim Delvoye, Stephanie Eckerskorn,
Marianne Esser, Matthias Flügge, Peter Foley, Brian Fox at
Swank, Alex Galloway, Jörg Gimmler, Adrienne Goehler, Lynn
Hollowell at Tandem Films, Gabriele Horn, Faith Hubley,
Hannah Hurtzig, Paul Johnson, Rainer Jordan, Norman Klein,
John Klima, Sergei Koladin, Jerzy Kucia, Marlies Krause,
Markus Krieger, Stefan Landwehr, Siegfried Langbehn,
Charlotte Laubard, Pia Lindman, Larissa van Loock, Kristin
Lucas, Judy Lybke, Niklas Maak, Kirsten Mayntz, Joe McKay,
Bernd Mehlitz, Zach Miner, Ralph Müller, Jason Nutt at
Pyramid Media, Carol Parkinson, Thomas Olbricht, Tony
Oursler, Ed Pusz, Karyn Riegel, Luminita Sabau, Dieter
Sauberzweig, Stefan Scherf, Imke Schwärzler, John Sirabella
and Rachel Gordon at the National Film Board of Canada, Zoran
Sinobad and Jerry Hatfield at the Library of Congress, Martin
Stadeli, Wolfgang Staehle, Iris Steinbeck, Karin Steinweh,
Holger Struck, Matten Vogel, Antje Vollmer, Hans-Georg Wieck,
Klaus Wowereit, Eric Zimmerman.